CONTENTS

1) Introduction to Harold Pinter — 1

2) Summary and Critical Analysis of The Homecoming — 10

3) Textual Analysis
   Act One — 13
   Act Two — 23

4) An Interpretation — 36

5) Character Analysis — 38

6) Pinter's Dramatic Techniques and Style — 50

7) The Comedies of Menace — 66

8) The Birthday Party — 69

9) The Dumb Waiter — 71

10) A Slight Ache — 72

11) The Caretaker — 74

12)	The Collection	76
13)	The Lover	78
14)	Overview	80
15)	Survey of Criticism	86
16)	Essay Questions and Model Answers	95
17)	Annotated Bibliography	110

BRIGHT NOTES

THE HOMECOMING AND OTHER WORKS BY HAROLD PINTER

Intelligent Education

Nashville, Tennessee

BRIGHT NOTES: The Homecoming and Other Works
www.BrightNotes.com

No part of this publication may be used or reproduced in any manner whatsoever without written permission, except in the case of brief quotations in critical articles and reviews. For permissions, contact Influence Publishers http://www.influencepublishers.com.

ISBN: 978-1-645421-80-1 (Paperback)
ISBN: 978-1-645421-81-8 (eBook)

Published in accordance with the U.S. Copyright Office Orphan Works and Mass Digitization report of the register of copyrights, June 2015.

Originally published by Monarch Press.
Steven H. Gale, 1971
2019 Edition published by Influence Publishers.

Interior design by Lapiz Digital Services. Cover Design by Thinkpen Designs.

Printed in the United States of America.

Library of Congress Cataloging-in-Publication Data forthcoming.
Names: Intelligent Education
Title: BRIGHT NOTES: The Homecoming and Other Works
Subject: STU004000 STUDY AIDS / Book Notes

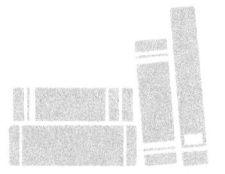

INTRODUCTION TO HAROLD PINTER

When Harold Pinter began his career as a dramatist in 1957, writing *The Room* at the request of a friend, he was a little-known actor in a touring repertory company. Nine years later he had been critically acclaimed "the most original, disturbing, and arresting talent in theatrical London" by the *London Sunday Times* and called "the most consistently successful serious dramatist of his generation," considered "not only the most inescapably haunting of our modern dramatists, but the most likely to survive as a permanent part of our dramatic literature," by the English critic John Russell Taylor. Pinter's dramas have received numerous awards, including the New York Critics' Antoinette Perry Award for the Best Broadway Drama of 1967 for *The Homecoming*, and Pinter himself was awarded the Order of the British Empire on the Queen's Birthday Honours List in 1966.

FAMILY AND EARLY LIFE

Pinter was born on October 10, 1930 in the Hackney section of inelegant East London. The only son of a Jewish tailor (questionably of Portuguese ancestry), the future playwright grew up in a world filled with vivid tales of the treatment of Jews in Hitler's Germany and literally had to fight his way home through gangs of young toughs during the post-war rise of neo-Nazism in England. The ever present aura of fear which he lived with became a basic element in his writing in later years.

SCHOOLING

Pinter won a scholarship to a local grammar school, Hackney Downs, where he was educated. His first experience with the theatre was seeing Sir Donald Wolfit in *King Lear*. In 1948 he entered the Royal Academy of Dramatic Arts, but did not find it to his taste, so he faked a nervous breakdown and left the Academy. He also stood two trials as a conscientious objector for refusing to join the National Service, for which he was fined a total of thirty pounds, the sum being paid by his parents.

ACTING CAREER

In 1949 Pinter began an eight year career as a repertory actor, travelling throughout Britain under the stage name of David Baron. During this time he spent eighteen months in Ireland with Andrew McMaster's touring company (fondly remembered in Pinter's Mac) and married the excellent British actress Vivien Merchant (1956). The couple have one child, a son, Daniel.

OVERVIEW OF PINTER'S WORKS

Pinter's plays compose a whole, each drama growing out of those which preceded it and leading into those which follow. A quick overview of his writing clearly shows his evolution as a dramatist from his earliest complete piece, *The Room*, which contains all of the elements to be found in his subsequent work, to *The Homecoming*, his latest major play and his best, in terms of both idea content and technique, as well as his most representative endeavor. Moreover, there is a discernible pattern which can be traced in Pinter's dramas, as he moves from discussing menace per se in the early plays to examining the source of that menace in his later plays.

THE COMEDIES OF MENACE

The first three plays, *The Room*, *The Birthday Party*, and *The Dumb Waiter*, collectively titled "comedies of menace," are essentially concerned with exposing the existence of personal menace in the world and charting the individuals destruction under the pressure of that menace. Problems in communication between individuals and the perception of reality (see the discussion of "verification" below) confront the characters in these early plays as they face omnipresent physical menace of undefined origin. One is reminded of the fear the author carried with him as a youth.

In *The Room* the menace merely exists, and the audience never finds out why - they are only presented with Rose's terror. *The Birthday Party* implies that society might be the source of menace, but nevertheless it is the menace and its effect which are important, not its derivation. *The Dumb Waiter* rounds out the picture of menace when the menacers are shown to be as susceptible to menace as those they terrorize.

PLAYS IN TRANSITION

The next two plays, *A Slight Ache* and *The Caretaker*, mark a shift in Pinter's emphasis as he begins to focus on the cause of menace rather than on the existence of menace itself. The actual shift involved is really quite simple. In *A Slight Ache* Pinter determines that the menace is not an external source which threatens a man and his wife, but an internal ingredient, based on the psychological needs of the individuals involved. In *The Caretaker*, Pinter's tale of two brothers and a tramp, psychological need as a motivating force is related to the actions of the characters.

THE LATER PLAYS

The Collection, *The Lover*, and *The Homecoming* continue the pattern begun with *A Slight Ache* and *The Caretaker*, as the dramatist extends his study of the origin of menace in psychological needs and demonstrates the drastic extents to which people will go in trying to satisfy their needs.

THE MAJOR WORKS

Introduction

In order to understand *The Homecoming* it is useful to survey Pinter's other works, for through them we can trace the thematic evolution which led to *The Homecoming*. The **themes** dramatist utilizes in this play are present from the very beginning (though they vary in the degree to which he has developed them from play to play).

Some reviewers, especially the early ones, have complained about the difficulty in understanding Pinter, but often the difficulty was a result of unfamiliarity with either the playwright's ideas, or his mode of expression, or both. Once again it is sometimes helpful to review the earlier plays, since many of them treat the same subjects in a more obvious manner, and it is always easier to find something if we know what we are looking for and have seen it before.

From the opening lines of *The Room* to the final curtain of Pinter's latest play, there are three concepts which to some degree lie behind each of the author's dramas. These three interrelated concepts-menace, communication, and verification -create the basic meaning of every Pinter work from the outset and serve simultaneously as both subjects and techniques in those works. Thus it is imperative to understand how Pinter defines each of these terms and then how he utilizes these concepts in his writing.

Essentially, every Pinter play can be seen as dealing with the three fundamental concepts in the following circular pattern. Menace exists, a priori. Because of the existence of menace there is a need for individuals to communicate with one another in order to gain reassurance, but the menace interferes and communication breaks down; or the individuals involved refuse to communicate for fear of exposing themselves to further menace. Lack of communication, therefore, ironically creates further menace. Because of the existence of menace there is also a need to verify things, to determine reality in other words. Unfortunately, menace again interferes and verification is hindered. The breakdown of communications further frustrates efforts to verify, and once more, additional menace is the result- which in turn produces a need for more communication and more verification, which cannot be met, reenforcing the menace, etc., etc. **Menace** Seldom defined in Pinter, menace is a threat to the status quo. Whereas in the early plays the threat is physical, it becomes progressively more psychological in nature in the succeeding dramas.

Menace, of course, comprises the subject matter of all the plays to some extent, whether it is the study of Rose's breakdown before the unknown horror represented by the basement in *The Room*, or Teddy's refusal to become emotionally involved with other human beings in *The Homecoming* because he fears that he will be rejected.

As a technique, Pinter relies on creating a mood of menace which carries the plot forward while at the same time it involves the audience with the suggestion that they are just as vulnerable to the terror embodied on stage as the characters are. The mood is neither surrealistic nor unfamiliar to the audience, for as Pinter claims in a March 3, 1960 B.B.C. European Service interview: "This thing, of people arriving at the door [unannounced, bringing terror with them], has been happening in Europe in the last twenty years. Not only the last twenty years, the last two to three hundred."

Communication

Pinter has specifically stated how and why he explores human failure in communications. In "Between the Lines," an article he wrote for the *London Sunday Times* in 1962, he explains his understanding of the functions of language and paralanguage. Quite obviously, according to Pinter, language is used to communicate; but it is also, and just as importantly, used for non-communication. In expanding on this idea, Pinter notes that language "is a highly ambiguous commerce. So often, below the words spoken, is the thing known and unspoken."

To the playwright's mind this realization leads to an observation about the two sorts of silence which can occur in speech:

There are two silences. One when no word is spoken. The other when perhaps a torrent of language is being employed. This speech is speaking of a language locked beneath it. . . . It is a necessary avoidance, a violent, sly, anguished or mocking smokescreen which keeps the other in its place. . . . One way of looking at speech is to say it is a constant stratagem to cover nakedness.

Obviously, of course, there can be silence when the characters (people) have nothing to say, but Pinter feels that more often silence, either the literal non-utterance of words or the "torrent of language," is employed to keep from saying anything. Clearly this use of language can be considered what would be categorized in psychological terminology as a defense mechanism-a means by which the individual organism tries to protect itself ("an unconscious mental process . . . that enables the ego to reach compromise solutions to problems," to use the words of *Webster's Seventh New Collegiate Dictionary*). The individual is not as likely to be attacked, at least not as likely to be successfully attacked, if he does not reveal his own weaknesses.

Equally clear to Pinter, the attempt to keep from saying anything is allied to his theory of verification (to be discussed immediately below):

There is another factor which I think has considerable bearing on the matter and that is the immense difficulty, if not the impossibility, of verifying the past. I don't mean merely years ago, but yesterday, this morning. What took place. ... If one can speak of the difficulty of knowing what took place yesterday one can I think treat the present in the same way. What's happening now? We won't know until tomorrow or six months' time, and we won't know then, we'll have forgotten, or our imagination will have attributed quite false characteristics to today . . . We will all interpret a common experience quite differently, though we prefer to subscribe to the view that there's a known ground. I think there's a shared ground all right, but that it's more like quicksand. Because "reality" is quite a firm word we tend to think, or to hope, that the state to which it refers is equally firm, settled and unequivocal. It doesn't seem to be, and in my opinion it's no worse or better for that.

It is difficult, if not impossible, under the circumstances Pinter describes, to talk about anything, since there seems to be no way to assess the meaning of anything. If, as the artist indicates in *The Dwarfs* for example, everybody is constantly changing, and changing to the extent that there is no such thing as a reference point because no one is recognizably the same person from one moment to the next, communication about oneself becomes impossible, let alone communication about things outside oneself.

Verification

The third tenet of Pinter's dramatic philosophy is that of verification. Once again the author has spoken openly about what he believes. In a program note for the original London performance of *The Room* and *The Dumb Waiter* in March, 1960, the author commented:

The desire for verification is understandable but cannot always be satisfied. There are no hard distinctions between what is real and what is unreal, nor between what is true or false; it can be both true and false. The assumption that to verify what has happened and what is happening presents few problems I take to be inaccurate. A character on the stage who can present no convincing argument or information as to his past experience, his present behavior or his aspirations, nor give a comprehensive analysis of his motives, is as legitimate and as worthy of attention as one who, alarmingly, can do all these things. The more acute the experience the less articulate its expression.

Verification and its effect on language are inseparable in Pinter's plays.

The implications of the statements quoted above are clear and serve as part of the fundamental subject matter of every play Pinter has written to date. The technique he uses to convert the idea of verification into dramatic terms is a very simple one. As John Russell Taylor has pointed out, the technique consists of "casting doubt upon everything by matching each apparently clear and unequivocal statement with an equally clear and unequivocal statement of its contrary." Or, as it is epitomized in *The Dwarfs* when one of the characters interrupts a long conversation with the completely irrelevant information that "I see that butter's going up," one can only agree with the second character when he replies, "I'm prepared to believe it, but it doesn't answer my question." The fact may be true, but it has no bearing on the matters at and. According to Pinter, maybe nothing can.

THE HOMECOMING AND OTHER WORKS

SUMMARY AND CRITICAL ANALYSIS OF THE HOMECOMING

SUMMARY OF THE ACTION

Act One

As the play opens, Max and Lenny, his middle son, seemingly almost come to blows as they verbally abuse one another. Sam, Max's brother, comes home from work and Max turns on him, berating him - bringing about a response about MacGregor. Joey, the youngest son, home from training at the gym, walks in and is included in Max's tirade. That night Teddy enthusiastically brings a hesitant Ruth home to meet his family after his six years' absence. Ruth leaves. Lenny enters. The brothers talk unconcernedly. Teddy exits. Ruth returns. She talks casually with Lenny while he fantasizes, then she "propositions" him. Ruth exits; Max enters and talks with Lenny. Next morning Joey, Max, and Sam continue their mutual abuse, discussing their strengths and weaknesses, when Teddy and Ruth enter. Max verbally attacks Ruth, then orders Joey to throw them out. When Joey refuses Max hits him, then prepares to embrace Teddy.

Act Two

Everybody relaxes at tea, Max talking about himself, Teddy, Lenny, and Ruth discussing philosophy. Teddy prepares to leave. Lenny and Ruth talk, then dance. Max and Joey return and Joey and Ruth engage in open loveplay. Ruth exhibits her command of the situation, forcing Teddy into discussing philosophy. Sam mentions MacGregor. Lenny and Teddy discuss cheese-rolls. Joey, returned from Ruth's bed, confronts his father and brothers. They discuss Ruth's staying. Ruth, returning, is invited to stay. They discuss terms, while Sam, objecting, collapses. Ruth agrees to stay. Teddy leaves for America and the family unit has been restructured as the curtain falls.

Dramatis Personae

Max - a man of seventy, the patriarchal ex-butcher in whose house the action takes place. Father of Teddy, Lenny, and Joey, and brother of Sam.

Lenny - a man in his early thirties who makes his living as a pimp; one of the more perceptive characters in the drama. Max's second son, brother of Teddy and Joey.

Sam - a man of sixty-three who fails at everything except being a chauffeur. Brother to Max.

Joey - a man in his middle twenties who works in demolition during the day and trains to be a boxer at night. Youngest son of Max and brother of Teddy and Lenny.

Teddy - a man in his middle thirties, a Ph.D. in philosophy who teaches at an American university; he has brought his wife home to meet his family. Max's oldest son and brother to Lenny and Joey.

Ruth - a woman in her early thirties, an ex-body model who has been married to Teddy for six years and who essentially controls the action of the play.

[Jessie - the dead mother who never appears, yet whose influence upon her family is overwhelming.]

THE HOMECOMING AND OTHER WORKS

TEXTUAL ANALYSIS

ACT ONE

SUMMARY TO THE ENTRANCE OF TEDDY AND RUTH

As the play opens, Max and Lenny, his middle son, seemingly almost come to blows as they verbally abuse one another. Sam, Max's brother, comes home from work and Max turns on him, berating him-bringing about a response about MacGregor. Joey, the youngest son, home from training at the gym, walks in and is included in Max's tirade.

Critical Analysis

This opening scene is extremely important in terms of: (1) setting the tone of the play; (2) beginning Pinter's dramatic expression of his interrelated concepts of menace, communication, and verification; (3) **foreshadowing** the development of his major **theme** concerning individual psychological needs as his character's motivating forces; and (4) displaying the dramatist's techniques.

Tone

It is immediately apparent that there is something wrong in the relationships between these men as they call each other names and threaten physical violence. The very intensity of their words and actions, not even considering the fact that they are a family unit and by definition should be close, creates a tension and feeling of menace. Indeed, the threatening mood of an underlying current of uncontrollable violence about to burst out upon the stage begins evolving from the moment Lenny and his father first speak.

Menace, Communication, and Verification

Reenforcing the feeling of menace deriving from the violent action is the realization that Max is trying to communicate with his sons and his brother, yet is unable to do so. The possibility of misunderstanding is added because of this lack of any real communication and this in turn enhances the chances that violence will become more than a threat. At the same time the **theme** of verification is brought out in the characters' speech, as when Max contradicts himself while delineating the attributes of his dead wife, Jessie, or when he carefully questions Sam about being the firm's best chauffeur. Nothing can be taken for granted, and if there can be no basic assumptions, it must mean that nothing is truly verifiable. This realization explains part of the problem of the lack of communication and simultaneously generates further feelings of menace (see the appropriate sections included in the "Introduction to *The Homecoming*" section above), since, as Pinter says, it is a human characteristic to demand some sort of firm hold on what is true or real (and, therefore, verifiable).

Individual Psychological Needs

Although it certainly is not clear this early in the drama just what is motivating the characters, there is a **foreshadowing** of the author's theme in the confrontations between the members of this family. The abnormal relationship existing between Max and Lenny, for instance, as expressed in their insults and threats, is part of a recurring pattern in the play in which the characters do verbal battle. While father/son rivalry is normal, the ritualized extent to which these men carry their game takes it beyond conventional limits. Because of the constant repetition of the pattern and since there seems to be no lasting grudge, we come to understand that the conflicts are partly serious, but also partly playful.

It is this idea of the "play" aspect of the confrontations which suggests that this is the only way the participants are capable of expressing their affections, a concept explored in Eric Berne's *Games People Play*. And, as Pinter comments in "Between the Lines," this formula prevents one from openly declaring his emotions, thus protecting him from possible rebuttal. The game-playing is needed because the individual psychological needs of the characters involved are not being met by others in the family (see *The Lover* and *The Collection* as previous examples of this): on the one hand these men are resorting to games in an attempt to find satisfaction for their needs, and on the other hand they are using the games as a defense mechanism, since those needs are not being fulfilled. Ironically, too, the games defeat the very purpose they were created to fulfill.

A feeling of menace created by and at the same time restrained by affection grows out of this situation. Max's role as a tyrannical old patriarch ruling a Freudian family unit is at least partly sustained by the consent of his sons, who have the intelligence (in the form of Lenny) and power (Joey) to overthrow him if they so desire. Conversely, he does not seriously try to expel them from his house. They all mock and threaten, but no one actually considers carrying out those threats, and the atrociously funny expletives Max applies to himself keep the action on a humorous level and indicate that the players are aware that they are immersed in a game. Again, the very existence of the game substantiates that psychological needs lie at the core of the individuals' actions, for it is the threat to the characters' mental well-being which has determined the nature of the game.

Techniques

The techniques Pinter uses to establish the meaning of this scene include: the utilization of realistic language to contrast with and thereby emphasize the failure of communication; the ignoring of statements and questions as part of the lack of communication; the contradictory and non-assumptive statements used to introduce the problem of verification; the creation of a mood of menace which grows out of such a background; the use of images of decay to expand the mood of uneasiness and menace; and the employing of humor (basically funny things said in an unfunny situation) as an element to contrast and thus heighten the tension of the action. These elements will be discussed more fully in the section on "Pinter's Style."

SUMMARY TO LENNY'S REENTRANCE

That night Teddy enthusiastically brings a hesitant Ruth home to meet his family after his six years' absence.

Critical Analysis

Pinter continues the introduction of elements and themes, now as related to Teddy and Ruth. Essentially, the function of this segment is simply to introduce the couple and to begin their characterization.

Teddy's Character

Teddy's overenthusiastic reaction to his returning to his father's home is remindful of the Queen's observation in *Hamlet* when she says, "The lady doth protest too much methinks." The vigor with which he tries to convince his wife that his family is composed of nice people who will welcome them warmly sounds more as if he is trying to convince himself. He has, in reality, come home seeking affection, but afraid that it will be denied him.

Ruth's Character

Ruth is hesitant because she is fearful that she will not fit, since she does not belong to the family - they do not even know that Teddy is married, as will come out in the next few scenes. Teddy talks to her as though she were a child, yet, **foreshadowing** later developments in which it will become obvious that not only is Teddy weak but also that Ruth is the strongest character in the play, she does not allow him to control her.

Themes

There is a lack of communication as Teddy fails to comprehend his wife's need to leave and Ruth does not understand her husband's need to stay, the psychological drive for affection which has motivated his return. Teddy's attitude in overstressing their need to stay continues the exposure of menace, because of his underlying fear of failure, as well as adding to the **theme** of verification because of the conflict between what he says and his manner of saying it (and his compulsion to state it in the first place).

SUMMARY TO MAX'S REENTRANCE

Ruth leaves. Lenny enters. The brothers talk unconcernedly. Teddy exits. Ruth returns. She talks casually with Lenny while he fantasizes, then she "propositions" him.

Critical Analysis

This sequence of events contains one of the most important series of conversation in *The Homecoming*. Not only are the author's basic concepts expanded upon, but, also, for the first time the characters' actions give a real clue to what motivates their extremely unconventional behavior.

Teddy And Lenny - An Uncommon Reunion

After Ruth proves her independence by leaving, Lenny reenters and one of the most unusual reunions in drama takes place, the significance of which has a great bearing on the meaning of the play as a whole. In spite of Teddy's previous assurances to his wife that his is a very warm, welcoming family, when he and Lenny meet after a complete separation that lasted six years, the two brothers calmly talk about inconsequential things as though they had dinner together only a few hours earlier. There is no surprise on Lenny's part at suddenly finding his long missing brother in the front room and neither brother betrays any emotional feeling as they converse. Indeed, it is not for several moments that mention of Teddy's absence is even made.

Lenny And Ruth - An Uncommon Introduction

When Teddy departs Ruth reappears and her initial meeting with her brother-in-law parallels the brothers' reunion in its strangeness. Once again there is no notice given to an extraordinary occurrence. Lenny talks to his brother's wife as if she were a normal part of the household, instead of recognizing that she is a strange woman who has just walked, unannounced and unaccounted for, into his living room.

Lenny's flights into fancy serve as additional examples of the verification **theme** while functioning as the "torrent" of speech which protects the speaker from the listener.

The fanciful tales are not adequate to protect him, though, and ironically the pimp who has been boasting about his imagined conquests of women finds his brother's wife making overt sexual advances toward him. The reversal catches him unawares and he can only stammer in dismay. Having proved her superiority in a game where her opponent made the rules, Ruth now retires.

Significance of The Unconventional

At first glance it may seem that the interreaction between Tedty and Lenny stems merely from their unwillingness to expose their emotional vulnerability, or, perhaps, from an embarrassment at being so overpoweringly in need of an emotional relation. Juxtaposing this occurrence with Lenny and Ruth's meeting, however, implies that the similarity in action bespeaks a similarity in motivation.

The realization that these people are so desperately in need of emotional attachments that they will accept any set of circumstances as normal, no matter how bizarre they may really be, on the off-chance that it may lead to their goals, reduces their behavior to an understandable and pathetic level.

SUMMARY TO THE END OF ACT ONE

Ruth exits; Max enters and talks with Lenny. Next morning Joey, Max, and Sam continue their mutual abuse, discussing their strengths and weaknesses, when Teddy and Ruth enter. Max verbally attacks Ruth, then orders Joey to throw them out. When Joey refuses, Max hits him, then prepares to embrace Teddy.

Critical Analysis

Prior to the entrance of the returning "Prodigal Son" and his wife, the prime importance of this section is the insight it provides into Max's character. As he insults Sam, his detailing of his life as one of hardship-caring for his ungrateful brother at his father's dying request and then raising his own family-makes his intolerance somewhat excusable.

In addition it certainly illuminates his reaction to Teddy's reappearance.

Max does not even address himself to Teddy initially (interestingly, Max, who has mentioned his ability to deal with animals, immediately recognizes Ruth's underlying character), and then when he does turn his attention on his son it is to make disparaging remarks about Ruth, suggesting that she is a whore. Following his downing of Joey, though, he determines that she is a mother and has raised three sons, as he has. Now that he has vented his emotions in physical rage, this common bond allows him to accept both her and her husband.

Max's Reactions

Here at the end of Act One is the first overt hint that the play's primary **theme** deals with the emotional requirements of the characters and their desperate attempts to find fulfillment, to gain psychological security. The father's first response is anger, and perhaps this is comprehensible when reviewed in conjunction with Max's immediately preceding tirade against his worthless brother, Sam, in which he delineates his assumption of responsibility and its consequences. Having sacrificed his life for his family, he can only see Teddy's going to America as desertion, a failure in his duty to his family.

But Max needs affection and consequently is willing to overlook Teddy's obligation-shirking, to forgive his son who loves his father enough to come home. The invitation to embrace as the first half of the play closes signifies Max's need through his offer and Teddy's need through his acceptance. The lines of affection have been reunited, temporarily at least.

FINAL COMMENT ON ACT ONE

At this point all of the important concepts and **themes** been established, preparing for everything that will happen in the second part of the play. It now remains for Pinter to present action which will allow his characters more clearly to expose their needs, draw all the lines together, and determine whether or not there is a satisfactory answer to the psychological predicament in which these individuals find themselves.

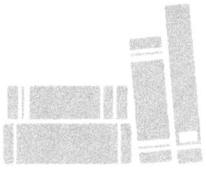

THE HOMECOMING AND OTHER WORKS

TEXTUAL ANALYSIS

ACT TWO

SUMMARY TO MAX'S GOING OUT

Everybody relaxes at tea: Max talking about himself; Teddy, Lenny, and Ruth discussing philosophy.

Critical Analysis

As Act Two of *The Homecoming* begins, some of the psychological background necessary for understanding the subsequent action is filled in. The characterizations of Max and Teddy are continued and Pinter's method of characterization, playing various personalities off against one another, also furnishes supplementary information about the natures of Lenny and Ruth, Most important to understanding the actions which conclude the play, and by extension provide the answer to the overall meaning of the drama, are the picture of the kind of man

Teddy is that is emerging and the hints gained about Ruth's attitude toward the kind of life she is living.

Max's Character

Max's reminiscences about his dead wife, Jessie, who taught her sons a moral (!) code to live by indicates that he is at ease. He enjoys having his family grouped around him and his pleasure leads to more remembering, this time about the closeness between himself and his sons when they were younger. The interlude is soon brought to an end, though, and his self-portrayal as a fond parent turns into a categorizing of the suffering he endured holding his large family together.

Teddy: Non-Perceptive and Mechanical

Teddy's glowing commentary on the good, happy roles he and Ruth fill in the university community contrasts sharply with his wife's ensuing description of an extremely stark existence and shows that he has no conception of how she feels about things - and perhaps he does not care. His actions at the end of the play only substantiate this. The picture of life in America expressed from Ruth's perspective, in turn, indicates why she feels free to choose as she does in the final action of the play.

 The reason for the husband's complete lack of understanding in regards to his wife becomes apparent in the three-sided discussion of philosophy in which this Ph.D. university Professor of Philosophy is out-philosophized by his pimp brother and his wife, a former body model. The answer to Teddy's character lies not in his inability to talk with Lenny and Ruth about his own topic, but his refusal to do so and the reason he gives later in the play for not even attempting to enter into a dialogue with them.

SUMMARY THROUGH THE LOVEMAKING SCENE

Teddy prepares to leave. Lenny and Ruth talk, then dance. Max and Joey return, and Joey and Ruth engage in open loveplay.

Critical Analysis

The Husband/Wife Relationship

When Teddy and Ruth first arrived, Teddy was very enthusiastic about staying in his father's house for several days, whereas Ruth was a bit hesitant. Now that Teddy sees that Ruth does fit into the family (in spite of her fears to the contrary and even in the face of his own assurances), he thinks that one night was long enough for a visit. At the conclusion of Act One, Ruth was accepted by right of having borne her husband three sons, and the tea break at the beginning of this act was so amiable that Teddy knows that, ironically, she has been made at home. She is, in fact, more at home in this sort of environment than she was in America, for it is much closer to the type of life she knew before she met and married Teddy. Any control which her husband might have been able to exercise over her heretofore has thus been nullified, and he wants to get her away so that he can regain his at best shaky, position of influence.

Ruth's Past

In talking with Lenny while Teddy is upstairs packing, Ruth admits that she used to work as a model. When Teddy comes back downstairs with the suitcases, Lenny has already recognized the kinship in thinking between Ruth and himself and is not willing to let her go without trying to establish some kind of relationship with her. This leads to one of the most hilariously bizarre - and to some, shocking-stage spectacles in English drama.

Lovemaking

When Joey and his father return from their outing, the dancing has ceased and the action has progressed to a long, drawnout kiss between Ruth and Lenny, while the husband/brother, Teddy, sits passively watching.

That Teddy is and remains a passive observer throughout the rest of this scene is probably what shocks most people, yet in terms of the way his character is developed, it is both understandable and logical. The reason behind his passivity lies in his history of failures in life which have reduced him to mechanical noninvolvement-which will be discussed below.

Meanwhile, Joey is so overcome by the exhibition taking place in front of him that he feels compelled to take part, too. And for the first time the family actually shows affection and tenderness as the two brothers caress their sister-in-law and their father stands by encouraging them. The extremely humorous situation reaches a **climax** as, to Max's admiring comments, the entwined couple rolls off the sofa.

Psychological Needs Exposed

This is, indeed, lovemaking of sorts and it is a prime example of how far those involved are willing to go in order to create a relationship with someone else. Their needs force them to commit acts which would normally be considered horrendous, but which become funny, partially because they seem so absurd, so exaggerated, and partially because the participants are reacting to such outlandish happenings as though they are common, everyday occurrences. Through these outrageous actions Pinter's characters are expressing their psychological needs much more effectively than would be possible through mere verbal statements.

SUMMARY TO JOEY'S COMING DOWNSTAIRS

Ruth exhibits her command of the situation, forcing Teddy into discussing philosophy. Sam mentions MacGregor. Lenny and Teddy discuss cheese-rolls.

Critical Analysis

Ruth's Command

The strength of Ruth's character is demonstrated by the ease with which she imposes her will on the members of this all-male household. Following the grotesquely funny tumble to the floor, Ruth asserts her superiority quite simply by demanding a drink of whiskey.

Lenny, who had earlier denied that there was any liquor in the house, obediently brings her some. Moreover, when Ruth refuses the drink unless it is put in a tumbler, her brother-in-law obligingly supplies one. Ruth has assumed a position of control; she is now the dominant figure.

Ruth And Teddy's Exposure

Having proved her control over her husband's family, Ruth now exerts herself over Teddy. Again, her exercise of control is subtly, unobtrusively shown - she allows him to expose himself, and simultaneously the reason for his inability to dominate his wife, by leading him into a seemingly irrelevant discourse on his philosophy.

Teddy's Philosophy

Teddy has never submitted his critical works to his own family, not because they would not understand them as a result of insufficient intelligence, but because they do not have the capacity to maintain intellectual equilibrium as he does.

What Teddy is saying is that he has managed to become detached from people and events to the extent that he can view them objectively. His subjective feelings do not enter into his observations. What this means in terms of Teddy's character is that he has become mechanical, dehumanized-he can now perceive people as objects and not become involved with them as people, on an emotional level. This is, of course, exactly what has just happened as he sat passively while his wife rolled around on the floor in Joey's unbrotherly embrace.

Teddy's Psychological Background

The reason for Teddy's retreat into this extreme form of objectivity is hinted at throughout the play, as his inability to form lasting relationships or control the people around him is demonstrated. A long history of failure has caused him to create a negative defense mechanism. If he sees people objectively, he does not need to fear rejection, since rejection can come only when there is emotional involvement - and how can an object present a threat? Teddy has constructed a shelter for himself by peopling the world in such a way that there is no possibility of communication or emotional entanglement, even as his very act of formulating this defense reveals his need for these elements.

A Preparative Interlude

In a brief exchange with his nephew, Sam manages to represent MacGregor in an implied derogatory manner, continuing to prepare for his revelation at the conclusion of the drama.

The Cheese-Roll

Lenny's accusation and Teddy's response in regards the stolen cheese-roll is a beautiful exemplification of Teddy's character, exposed bare moments earlier. His background of failure has reduced him to the point that his only effective form of revenge lies in pinching his younger brother's cheese-roll.

SUMMARY TO RUTH'S COMING DOWNSTAIRS

Joey, returned from Ruth's bed, confronts his father and brothers. They discuss Ruth's staying.

Critical Analysis

In the absurd dialogue which develops when Joey comes downstairs after having been with his sister-in-law for several hours, the extent of the desperation within the various characters becomes even clearer. The key is their treating Ruth as an object (more so than Teddy had previously), rather than as a human being. Her existence is important to them only in relation to how well she can fulfill their needs, and their perceptions of her are geared solely toward the goal of self-satisfaction.

Joey's Confession

In a "touching" scene of brotherly concern, Joey admits to his older brothers that he has failed to culminate his relationship with Ruth sexually.

Sex as A Medium of Expression

Joey's confession is a salient feature of the play, not only as a characterizing device relating to the boxer, but also in terms of understanding what the play itself means. The action seems to be an expression of sexual desires, with Ruth the immediate object through which the men may satisfy themselves. An interpretation of the play on this level, however, would fail to explain Joey's lack of disappointment or frustration at not having achieved sexual consummation. As he says, one need not always go all the way to find satisfaction. He obviously was psychologically in need of something other than a sexual relationship, and his attitude toward Ruth as the drama ends suggests that he has accepted her as a replacement for his dead mother.

The Birds in The Scrubs

Pinter's **theme** of verification comes to the surface again when Teddy insinuates that his brother's failure was due to a lack of ability. Lenny leads Joey through what is probably an apocryphal tale, the veracity of which is suspect because of Joey's continual hesitations. The story serves also as further evidence, therefore, of Lenny's imagination. And it is further evidence that Lenny's power over women is questionable-it would seem that he has to rely on imaginative stories (see his earlier account to Ruth) and partake vicariously through his brother's experiences in order to assert himself.

Max's Return

Max is upset that his boy has been frustrated in his attempt with Ruth, which leads him to the thought that it might be a good idea to keep a woman around the house to fulfill whatever functions they can find for her.

The Debate

Teddy, who had tried before to persuade his wife that she would like staying with his family, reverses himself, now opining that it might be better if she returned to America, since she is not well. This is about the extent of his resistance. Sam offers the objection that she ought to return to her three children, but both he and his favorite nephew are ignored. That Ruth is not meant to remain as a member of the family becomes evident with Max's statement that they will have to pay her. The decision has been made-actually, it was really a foregone conclusion at the moment that it was suggested.

Business

Having agreed to supply her with money, and other human considerations, the family ironically asks Teddy how much he is willing to put into the kitty to help support his wife. Teddy surprises his father by refusing to donate to the cause. This, in turn, brings forth the suggestion from Lenny that it might be a better idea if he used his professional talents to set her up as a prostitute so that she could help support herself.

SUMMARY TO THE CONCLUSION

Ruth, returning, is invited to stay. They discuss terms, while Sam, objecting, collapses. Ruth agrees to stay. Teddy leaves for America and the family unit has been restructured as the curtain falls.

Critical Analysis

All of the psychological threads are woven together in this concluding segment of the play, the actions of each of the characters in *The Homecoming* becoming understandable as efforts to fulfill personal needs.

Crisis: Teddy Extends The Invitation

On Ruth's reentrance the play comes to a crisis point as Teddy informs his wife of the family's invitation for her to remain behind with them. Had Ruth decided to return with her husband, of course, the drama would have taken on a very different meaning, but Pinter wants to stress the desperation of his characters, so Ruth elects to stay.

Interestingly enough, Teddy has nearly accepted defeat, in spite of the minimal resistance he has offered to the family's proposal, for he assures his wife that they can get along without her at home. The final opposition that he manages to muster comes when he explains that she would be expected to help financially, since the economic situation is a little bit tight-he reminds her of the alternative (ironically), returning home with him, which she completely ignores.

A Settlement

At this point Lenny tells her the conditions of her employment, and she enters into collective bargaining with her hosts in which she counters their offers with her demands. Everybody is quite businesslike during the negotiations, and the talk in contractual terminology is amusing, considering the subject. Ruth is a tough bargainer, as might be expected, and manages to obtain all of the concessions she wants in an entirely emotionless manner. The lack of emotion carries over into the succeeding sequence of events, once more emphasizing the extreme personal involvement of the characters which effectively prevents them from interest or concern about the well-being of anyone else.

Sam's Collapse

In a final endeavor to stop things, to shock everyone back into a more normal perspective, Sam reveals that Jessie and her husband's best friend, MacGregor (he of the veiled references), made love in the back seat of his cab while he was there. He then falls to the floor and lies motionless.

Sam has been trying to protect Jessie's "good" name during the entire course of the drama. Why, then, does he attempt to discredit her at this point? In love with his sister-in-law to the point of excusing her indiscretions, Sam does not want to see anyone come into the house who might take Jessie's place, and he rightfully sees that Ruth will do just that. He attempts, therefore, to discredit his idealized love in hopes that the revelation will appall everybody, and, thus, preserve the status quo. Unfortunately, nobody in this family is shockable.

The reactions of the family are indicative of their total self-centeredness. Joey and Lenny calmly observe that their uncle is not dead. Max, at first upset that his brother is cluttering up the room, becomes angrier when he realizes that Sam is such a failure that he cannot even die correctly. Teddy, his uncle's favorite nephew (and this is possibly a second motive for Sam's behavior), is concerned only with the inconvenience this will cause him-he had planned on Sam's driving him to the airport and now he will have to find some other means of transportation. Ruth does not bother to acknowledge that anything has happened at all.

Teddy's Departure

There is nothing left to keep Teddy here any longer, so he leaves. As he goes, though, to the friendly goodbyes of his brothers, two things happen which yet again underscore the **theme** of personal need. First, his father sends a photograph of himself to his grandson-he has nothing against Teddy, but then he can dismiss his oldest son as someone who fills no service for him and is thereby rendered unimportant. Second, Ruth shows a similar lack of either animosity or concern when she tells him not to become a stranger.

The Family Portrait

With Teddy's exit the play draws to a close. Ruth has been kept by the family to satisfy their needs, but it has already been established that she is the strongest personality in the drama and it is evident that her staying will fill her personal requirements. They mean to use her, but it is she who will do the using.

All of this is evident in the stylized scene as the curtain falls. Ruth sits in a chair, caressing Joey's head as he kneels at her feet, his head in her lap; Sam lies still on the floor on one side of her; Max, beginning to realize who is truly in control, is on his knees at her other side; Lenny stands silently watching. It is a traditional family portrait.

THE HOMECOMING AND OTHER WORKS

AN INTERPRETATION

After being exposed to *The Homecoming*, an audience is likely to be filled with questions, chief among them being, "What is the meaning of the play?" and "How can a husband sit still while his wife is being treated like that?" (i.e., the play is not very realistic, is it?).

Obviously, there are many **themes** which run through this drama: the three basic **themes** of menace, verification (involving the traditional reality vs. appearance), and communication; sex; domination; and individual psychological needs. It is this last item which really holds the key to all questions asked about *The Homecoming*, because an understanding of the play in this perspective incorporates the various sub-themes and explains all the actions which take place during the course of the drama.

As has been demonstrated in the foregoing "Critical Analysis," each of the characters is driven by a need to satisfy certain requirements for his own mental well-being (specifics relating to the individual characters will be treated in a later section, "Character Analysis"). Taking this motivation into account, the actions of the characters, while desperate, become understandable, since everything can be seen as being devoted toward that end. With the three basic themes, then, menace arises from the unfulfilled needs, and problems in verification and communication are symptoms of the underlying quest for satisfaction. Sex and domination are the means employed by Max, Teddy, Ruth, Lenny, Joey, and even Sam in their attempts to procure whatever it is that they specifically require.

When asked by Henry Hewes, in an interview/play review for the *Saturday Review*, what *The Homecoming* is about, Pinter answered, "It's about love and lack of love. The people are harsh and cruel, to be sure. Still, they aren't acting arbitrarily but for very deep-seated reasons." When applied to *The Homecoming* this statement explains much of why the characters do what they do. The need to love and to be loved, a primary appetite (see the "**Introduction to** *The Homecoming*" for an explanation of this term), is at the core of all the characters' actions. It is also the cause of all their troubles. Asked whether the family represents evil, Pinter contends, "There's no question that the family does behave very calculatedly and pretty horribly to each other and to the returning son. But they do it out of the texture of their lives and for other reasons which are not evil but slightly desperate." If, as suggested above, the people in the drama are desperate in their needs, then everything they do may be aimed at satisfying themselves. This would explain how they can do some of the things they do to one another.

THE HOMECOMING AND OTHER WORKS

CHARACTER ANALYSIS

The meaning of *The Homecoming* is most easily understood when one finds out why the characters act the way they do: what do they want (or need) and how are their actions designed to gain them satisfaction?

Max

Max, Sam, Joey, and Lenny are involved in round-about approaches in their continual battle for emotional security, and the things they do are either aimed at their goals or are derived from their frustration at a lack of achievement. Max's past was not an especially happy one, and he has continually been placed in roles which demand respect, though not affection, from those he rules as the old patriarch in a Freudian primal family unit. This is demonstrated in his humorously exaggerated accounts of his duties, which include earning money for psychiatrists, and so forth. From the time of Jessie's death he has been both mother (cooking) and father to his sons. Although he admits that there have been no women in his house since his wife died, he does crave affection, as when he welcomes Teddy back at the end of Act One and again at the beginning of Act Two when his mellow conversation with his family indicates that they are important to him; he shows concern when he finds out that Joey has been teased by Ruth; he is eager to have his daughter-in-law stay to become a part of the family; he wonders if Teddy's sons would enjoy a photograph of their grandfather. Whether he acts toward his family the way he does because he cannot accept affection or whether he has foregone that emotion in order to keep his family together is difficult to ascertain.

Max is beginning to show the insecurity of old age and fears that he may be too old for anyone to be interested in him - he continually asks Ruth if she thinks he is too old for her - and perhaps he sees his daughter-in-law as being able to provide him with the attention he has been deprived of, as well as proving that he is not too old. Whatever the reason, it is Max who first suggests that it might be a good idea to have her stay.

Sam

In contrast to his brother, Sam is a ne'er-do-well who apparently has never been able to get close to anyone. He did not care enough to follow his father's trade as a butcher and has been unable to produce anything on his own, for which Max taunts him. As a chauffeur, he merely serves the commands of others.

Sam's ineffectualness may have grown out of his feelings for his sister-in-law, Jessie, and his comments throughout the play indicate that he is tied to his brother's late wife in some way or another. They also indicate that he loved her-possibly the only simple and sincere expression of love to be found in *The Homecoming*. Yet this love is questionable too. Although he knows that she was unfaithful, he acknowledges that there is no other woman in the world who could compare favorably with her. Is he talking about Jessie's attributes, or, perhaps, is he making a comment about women in general? Perhaps Sam is retreating from any intimate contact with women by adhering to an idealized picture of Jessie. Being dead, she cannot test his devotion or ability as a live woman might.

Whatever the case, the uncle is tied to his idealized memories of the dead woman and even though he witnessed her infidelity with her husband's best friend, no one can take her place. Sam's collapse at the end of the drama might be an attempt, on the other hand, to protect Jessie, even though he has to tarnish her memory in the process. By introducing the shocking information about her affair he may hope to keep the family from replacing Jessie with Ruth.

Joey

Joey is a figure of impotence. He can create nothing, working in demolition during the day and training as a boxer at night. As a boxer he is not an overpowering figure, as described with wonderful accuracy when Max defines Joey's inept fighting style as a combination of the inability to attack and the inability to defend.

As a lover, too, Joey is a failure. He had to be led through the story of his latest exploit with a bird near the Scrubs and then, although he initiated the action with Ruth, he had her up in his room for two hours without sexual consummation. Joey does not seem overly upset by his lack of success. He just does not want anyone else to get the credit, not even the woman's own husband.

Jessie filled many roles in her relations with the members of the household, and it may well be that Joey turns to Ruth as a substitute mother, since Jessie is gone. If so, he would not look to his sister-in-law as a source of sexual satisfaction. This would explain his lack of concern over not going all the way and is suggested as the play concludes when he kneels at Ruth's chair to be petted. He is really only a little child in his appetites.

Lenny

Lenny is shown to be incapable of satisfactorily coping with situations in which women are involved. His tales of mastery over women, his reliance on Joey as a surrogate through which he succeeds vicariously, and his relations with Ruth all indicate that he is not likely to achieve true success in adventures with the opposite sex.

Lenny's flights into fancy concerning women display his lack of emotional equilibrium. His account of the lady who made him a certain proposal is so farfetched (including the **cliches** and the ridiculous practicality of not committing murder in spite of the propitious circumstances because he did not want to get into a state of tension) that it is humorous. Ruth's question about how he knew the lady was diseased and his answer that he decided that she was make the whole story even more amusing, but it also introduces a more serious note, relating it both to Pinter's **theme** of verification and implying Lenny's view of women. It makes no difference what the truth of the matter is, whether the girl did indeed have the pox, all that is important is how the characters react to a given statement. Ruth reflects the desire for verification, even though the fact is insignificant in terms of the action completed, and Lenny's answer implies that something can be both true and false simultaneously-while there is no evidence that his pursuer was diseased, his actions are the same as if she were, and he rejects her-a symbolic subconscious rejection of all women.

Starting with his own mother, and then by virtue of his profession, Lenny has been exposed to a low order of women, and the only woman for whom he has ever felt affection left him-his mother died. Unable to accept women because he would be vulnerable to desertion again, he rejects them violently in a protective reflex (a defense mechanism, as defined above), to keep himself free from emotional entanglements even as he seeks them.

A clue to Lenny's stories of conquest over women and his actions in the drama is given when Ruth calls him Leonard and he asks her not to use that name because his mother gave it to him. Jessie has been dead for an indefinite number of years (more than six, at the very least, since the living room wall had been torn down after her death, and prior to Teddy's departure for America), yet her presence is powerfully felt on stage throughout the entire drama as she is referred to by every member of the family and her memory affects the actions of each individual in some way or another. That Lenny finds it difficult to establish a normal relationship with women is obvious. This may be due to any of the reasons previously noted, or it may stem from his comparison of women to the standard of his mother (like Sam, he can find no one who is her equal, so he does not even want to be referred to by the name she gave him), or from his mother's overwhelming and stifling power over him-maybe he just does not want to be called Leonard because he did not like his mother.

Even Ruth is a threat to him. Lenny is amused that he is in his pajamas and Ruth is fully clothed when they first meet, since this is a reversal of his normal working conditions, and he jokingly calls attention to the fact. When things start to get serious, however, he can only retreat in confusion, a retreat which lasts for the rest of the play. Or at least until he is secure in the knowledge that Ruth is no threat to him because she is not interested in a relationship in which emotions would be involved.

Teddy

Teddy's actions provide another means of exploring the **theme** suggested by his not exhibiting his ability in philosophical matters. Lenny and Teddy, joined by Ruth, discuss the nature of the universe, the question of what is true versus what is not true. As in Lenny's story of the girl with the pox, it is again not the validity of the premise that is important but the actions stemming from it. The professor's brother (a pimp) and wife (a former body model) better demonstrate an understanding of his subject than he does. Lenny is aware of a philosophical question and the words on which to phrase it; Teddy does not respond in the same vein. When Ruth enters the fray, it is to introduce a new perspective.

Throughout Pinter's works there is a pattern of individuals failing in other areas of their lives as a reflection of their lack of success in creating viable relationships with their companions (Davies in *The Caretaker* and Edward in *A Slight Ache* are just two prime examples of this typical Pinter character type). While he may simply not wish to discuss his interests with a layman, his chosen profession would be the one area in which Teddy should be able to exhibit his proficiency. However Teddy proves himself capable of doing little besides stealing cheese-rolls. And there are ample instances in which he meets defeat in the drama, as in his inability to control Ruth in the opening scenes of the first act.

Teddy may be a material success, he is a professor who is paid enough to take his wife to Europe, but Pinter is not interested in material success in any of his plays.

It is possible that Teddy is actually a success as a philosopher, for he faces all situations with a philosopher's equanimity, while still not being able to solve essential problems such as meeting his wife's psychological requirements or maintaining a lasting relationship with his father and brothers which will fulfill his own emotional needs.

Whether or not Teddy has failed in his profession, it is certain that he did not succeed in his return home. He enters the house full of hope and leaves without his wife. No emotional ties have been re-established-indeed, some have been nullified. Teddy's failure in returning spills over into his marriage, and his own family disregards the fact that Ruth is his wife. As the couple is about to depart for America, Teddy's family demonstrates the overwhelming sense of selfish motivation they have which is partly responsible for their alienation. The hilarious farce of the lovemaking scene taking place in front of the non-objecting husband produces the evidence and at the same time the expression of Teddy's failure. His reaction to his wife's performance suggests that he has been led to expect failure. If he has failed in his relations with his father and his brothers, there is no reason to expect success in his marriage, so Ruth's actions come as no real surprise. The rest of the family's easy acceptance of the events as entirely natural indicates their attitudes toward one another, for they are too interested in how events affect them personally to be able to look at a situation with sympathy for the participants. Teddy is not important to them as a person.

Teddy's response to Ruth's question of whether his family has read any of his works reveals a lack of communication and an attempt to find refuge or shelter on an intellectual level, though his failure to answer Lenny's philosophical questions has already suggested that he is not merely detached as he claims, but possibly incapable. He cannot express his feelings to his brother when they are reunited after six years' separation. Ties of affection seem beyond him, since his connections with his father, brothers, uncle, and wife are superficial (no one is truly pleased at his return and Ruth is ready to stay behind), so he no longer expresses interest in participating, though his initial re-union with his father implied desire for acceptance. The contrast in Teddy's attitude at the beginning of the drama and his attitude at its conclusion illustrates his inability to form lasting bonds as well as reflects his recognition of his failure- he returns home so eagerly, yet soon becomes anxious to leave, having established no relationships with his family, unmoved by his uncle's collapse, and having lost his wife. Only by removing himself from the sphere of human emotion can he face his condition.

Teddy's weakness is that he can feel emotion, but cannot excite a reciprocal feeling in those about him. That he was happy to get home was shown in his trying to convince Ruth that his family would welcome them: he pointed out his father's chair to his wife, specifically mentioned greeting his father in the morning, seemed pleased that they would surprise the old man and assured Ruth that she would like him. After he was greeted by Lenny, Teddy asked about his dad. When father and son finally meet at the end of Act One, Teddy is ready for the embrace proposed by his father.

Unfortunately, his talks with the family prove that he cannot communicate, and events in the play show that he has no control over anybody. Since he can control no one, Teddy views people as pieces of machinery so that he will not have to relate to them on a personal level, a classic example of the defense-by-withdrawing mechanism. Because he sees everyone as a machine, he feels no emotion toward them and can simply observe their movements, a case of defense by restructuring the world (autism - the tendency to see things as we want to see them). He is the furthest removed from the human sphere of the family members (the only real threat he poses is to cheese-rolls, and he inhumanly views his family as objects) and cannot even take part in the game anymore.

Ruth

Biblically the faithful wife, Ruth has not been satisfied by her husband or children and seeks attention from her husband's family. The realizations fostered by Teddy's "objects" speech in Act Two are foreshadowed in his treatment of Ruth at the beginning of the drama. He apparently regards her as a child or an object, and probably has for some time. Ruth asks his permission to sit down, for instance, and he tries to send her to bed because she needs some rest. This manner of treatment certainly cannot be satisfactory for a mature individual, so Ruth is in a position to seek a more fulfilling relationship elsewhere. As a result of her starvation for acceptance as the person she is, a woman with desires and emotions, and her need for emotional stimulation on that level, Ruth is forced to disregard socially approved sources of these elements.

Pinter points out that, "If this had been a happy marriage, it wouldn't have happened. But she didn't want to go back to America." There is evidence in the play that Ruth has not been happy in her marriage. The first clue to this fact is Teddy's attitude toward his wife when they are originally introduced, an attitude reflected in his treating her as an object or a young child rather than as a mature woman. It should also be remembered what her previous occupation was and that by her own admission she was not the same when she first met Teddy. Teddy apparently has forced her into a new and alien role, that of a university professor's wife. Teddy's description of Ruth's role in their life in America is appropriately attractive; Ruth's description of America as a bare, sterile place differs markedly, indicating that her life there has not been so rosy. It is clear from the picture she presents that she has been living a lonely, barren life. That Teddy misunderstands his wife is demonstrated when he tries to convince her to return with him by reminding her that she can help him with his lectures when they get back.

Ruth's present surroundings are much closer to the type of environment she would be at home in than the situation existing in the United States. "The woman is not a nymphomaniac as some critics have claimed," declares Pinter. "...She's in a kind of despair which gives her a kind of freedom. Certain factors like marriage and the family for this woman have clearly ceased to have any meaning." Since marriage and the family have failed to satisfy her primary appetites, they are not fulfilling their functions and may be discarded. Pinter would disagree with critics who call the play absurd or unrealistic, too. The basic premise of a woman who will turn to any one in an attempt to find affection is not absurd in the author's world picture. The motivation for the actions takes them out of the realm of the absurd. Women who are driven to this point by their desperation are not harlots in the sense of selling themselves for money or even for sexual pleasure - they are driven by a need to fill deep emotional voids. Ruth's description of America has already indicated that for the past six years she has been a very lonely woman in what are for her sterile surroundings.

While the conclusion of the play is astonishing if taken out of context, as in the "comedies of menace," the movement from a realistic beginning has been smooth and logical, each step being a bit more absurd than the one before it, yet it is based on its predecessor. Where many people suffer the same fate as Ruth, few of them handle their problems as well: Pinter notes that she has been "used by this family. But eventually she comes back at them with a whip. She says, 'if you want to play this game I can play it as well as you.' She does not become a harlot. At the end of the play she's in possession of a certain kind of freedom. She can do what she wants, and it is not at all certain she will go off to Greek Street. But even if she did, she would not be a harlot in her own mind." What Pinter is claiming is that Ruth has been placed outside conventional boundaries by the failure of traditions such as marriage to meet her requirements, so that anything she does to meet her requirements is acceptable to her if it brings her closer to satisfaction. This is demonstrated in her businesslike bargaining over the details of her contract and place of work-when they are talking about setting her up as a prostitute.

Because of the circumstances and her motivation, Ruth does not fit the traditional definition of a harlot (no one in the play ever reaches a sexual culmination with her, after all). The whole play is epitomized in Ruth's farewell to her husband. She feels no real affection, antipathy, or guilt toward him-she has done what she had to do. In the power struggle Ruth is the strongest; new lines of attachment are established, and at the end of the play she sits with her new family arranged about her as in a traditional family portrait.

THE INCLUSIVENESS OF THE CHARACTERIZATIONS:

There is no need for Pinter to deal with either nature or society as specific entities in *The Homecoming*, since the family contains within its makeup the things which are nature and society. Esslin has suggested in *The Peopled Wound* that all of the characters are somehow connected with the underworld, but this would seem to limit the application of the meaning of the play as a whole. On the contrary the family unit provides the circumstances in which variations on several **themes** may be experimented with. A philosopher and a chauffeur do not have the vitality to stand up to the life forces of a butcher, a pimp, and a boxer, who in turn fall before a woman's sexual wiles. Ironically, these "vital" elements are impressive only in comparison with Teddy and Sam The provider of food has been tricked by a gang of crooks so the family has to skimp to get by; the procurer is unable to fill his own demands, and the fighter is not a physical threat to anybody.

Nevertheless, each level of living comes closer to the primal components of life itself: Teddy and Sam can exist only in an already created civilization; Max, Lenny, and Joey represent elements (food, sex, battle) necessary to forge a society with enough leisure and ease to permit philosophers and chauffeurs (unessential thought, luxury) to exist, and Ruth is the element out of which life is created, and is, therefore, the most important and strongest of all forces, for she is closest to the basic drives of life (without which the others have no meaning).

THE HOMECOMING AND OTHER WORKS

PINTER'S DRAMATIC TECHNIQUES AND STYLE

For the most part, Pinter's dramatic techniques are very simple, and much of his success as a dramatist is based on this simplicity. In the early plays he used blackouts and what he has called "cabaret turns" to mystify his audience and to underscore his main points. With the later dramas, however, he allows his main points to determine his mode of expression. This is especially true in *The Homecoming*.

The structure, the dramatic expression of the concept of verification, the use of humor, and the "Pinteresque" employment of language ("Pinterese") in *The Homecoming* not only create a distinctive style, but also are essential in conveying and carrying the meaning of the drama. Quite often several of these elements are used in conjunction with one another, either as the means of carrying the meaning or as the actual statement of meaning. Humor, for example, is used for specific reasons, just as language is, but the special use of language is also a source of humor, so that both elements fulfill Pinter's purpose of, say, exposing problems in communication and the resultant situation. They function simultaneously as the statement and the means of expressing the statement. The tightness and economy of the resulting play, together with a reconciliation and balancing of diverse elements creates a harmonic effect, a sense of orchestration so tangible that critics recognize the poetic, musical nature not only of the dialogue, but also of the piece in its entirety with its thematic overtones and resonant elements.

STRUCTURE

The basic structural device in the play is the framework of a power struggle, in which sex turns out to be the deciding agent. In a series of skirmishes throughout the drama, the characters meet, compete, and attempt to gain dominance over one another, with Ruth using sex to emerge victorious. There is a tension set up by the alternating tonalities (humor versus horror, for example) of the continuing confrontations.

Through the form of verbal fencing, the weaponry of the power struggle, Pinter exposes the characters and their beliefs, thus providing the meaning of the play. For instance, Teddy and Lenny's discussion of the dual nature of reality can in part be considered a battle for position, but it is also important as a means for discovering some of the characters' individual problems. Teddy, the professional philosopher, fails to solve problems in his own field. Lenny practices logical thinking on his own to devise theoretical answers, establishing his superiority over his older brother, thereby making more concrete their personal identities. Ruth begins with Lenny's assumptions, but rejects them by applying the principle of practicality, reducing them to an emotional level - the level on which they actually function anyway. And so it is throughout the play.

VERIFICATION

As mentioned above (see "**Introduction to** *The Homecoming*"), Pinter's technique for dramatically expressing his concept of verification is extremely simple. He merely juxtaposes mutually-contradictory statements of fact. Max's contrasting descriptions of his dead wife, Jessie; Lenny's decision about the girl falling apart with the pox; Joey's story about the birds in the Scrubs; Sam's approval of Jessie as a woman without peer and his exposure of her infidelity; and the conflict in the descriptions of America offered by Teddy and Ruth are all examples of this technique.

HUMOR

Pinter's humor contains many of the normal elements of humor, mostly verbal in nature: puns, non sequiturs, jokes, wit, and even a Yiddish phrasing. These are included for the common reasons: plain humorous effects, characterization, contrast, relief, and so forth. For instance, after Max has referred to Jessie's "rotten stinking face," which made him sick just to look at it, he labels himself a "lousy filthy father." The immediate intention, aside from the simple humor involved in someone calling himself lousy and filthy, is to take the sting out of the original description of Jessie.

Since it is doubtful that Max intends his description of himself to be taken literally, the unflattering picture of his wife can be ignored, too. Of course, in keeping with Pinter's methods, he may have been speaking the truth in both cases.

But the most important aspect of humor in *The Homecoming* is that which grows out of the meaning of the play or the concepts which underlie it. Pinter himself has commented on the element of humor to be found in his dramas and his comment indicates the close relationships between the use of this device and the meaning of his plays:

> Everything is funny; the greatest earnestness is funny; even tragedy is funny. And I think what I try to do in my plays is to get to this recognizable reality of the absurdity of what we do and how we behave and how we speak. The point about tragedy is that it is no longer funny. It is funny, and then it becomes no longer funny ... the fact that it is verging on the unknown leads us to the next step, which seems to occur in my plays. There is a kind of horror about and I think that this horror and absurdity go together.

This situation produces a kind of humor which basically derives from funny things said in unfunny situations. Lack of communication and the inability to verify things sometimes lead to this sort of humor, though more often it hearkens back to the psychological basis of the drama - the characters have reached the stage of desperation where they are perfectly willing to accept anything as though it were normal, any action by another character, no matter how absurd that action might be, on the chance that it will lead to a relationship which will satisfy their emotional needs. Examples of this are the first meetings in the play between Teddy and Lenny and then between Lenny and Ruth. No outward notice of the strangeness of the events is taken by any of the participants.

Similarly, the psychological problems of the individuals involved contribute to this type of humor. Thus Teddy sits impassively, making the spectacle of his wife and brother rolling around on the floor hilarious; If he is not upset, why should the audience become emotionally involved in the action? And without emotional involvement, the absurdity of the happening can be appreciated. Likewise, Max's reaction to the information that Ruth has denied Joey is not one of horror at the event or concern for the duty imposed upon woman, but a wonderment that his son could have been treated in such a cavalier manner. He is too concerned with his own selfish desires to identify with another person.

LANGUAGE

Pinter's use of language is the most distinctive device in his collection of dramatic tools. The dialogue in the author's plays has been called musical because of the sounds of the words, the phrasing, the rhythm, and the measured pauses and silences. It has also been called rhapsodic because of the partial statements, and near repetitions which form sub-themes throughout the individual pieces and the non sequiturs which indicate, as counterpoints, where the individual's speaker attention is really focused. Pinter has repeatedly explained (see his comments on the nature of language in our "Introduction to *The Homecoming*," for example) that language and the non-use of language can both be utilized for either communication or non-communication, either consciously or unintentionally. His ability to reproduce human speech more faithfully than a tape-recorder has led to his dialogue being called realistic or even superrealistic, the term superrealistic meaning that, although he does not reproduce common speech exactly, he has captured its essence so perfectly that it seems more real than actual speech.

The reason that Pinter's dialogues sound so real is that he has realized that traditional stage conversations are too stylized, too logical in structure as well as content. In real life people do not or cannot impart the amount of information as they are pictured as doing in the average stage play. Furthermore, as Pinter points out, expression under the influence of the emotions is not likely to be especially logical and may in fact become unintelligible. An Iago finds it much easier to express himself clearly and effectively than does an emotionally involved Cassio. As a dramatist, Pinter has put this recognition into practice.

Besides merely reproducing natural-sounding word-patterns on stage and appealing to the audience by having his characters speak in the same way his audience does, Pinter also uses realistic language to contrast with, and emphasize, events which take place on the stage. Typically in Pinter there is always a current of realistic speech which runs through his plays. Typically there is also a current of absurdity. It has been explained above that the absurdity is magnified when seen only as an end product, that a careful tracing of the movement from event to event shows a fairly logical progression. Everything which happens is a bit more absurd than whatever preceded it, but is logically derived from the preceding circumstances. The progression of Pinter's plays, then, appears to be a movement from reality (reading a newspaper) to absurdity (a wife staying behind with her husband's family in order to become a prostitute, with no real objection on the part of the abandoned husband-or abandoning husband). The underlying current of realistic language all the while contrasts with the "unrealistic" context of events in which it is uttered. In addition this contrast emphasizes the absurdity of the context so that it seems even more absurd than it might otherwise appear. The fact that the characters speak as though engaged in everyday conversation in the midst of these outrageous happenings underscores the non-normal aspects involved. This is one of the prime functions of Pinter's realistic dialogue.

The techniques the dramatist employs to create his realistic dialogue are many and varied: (A) cliches. (B) jargon, (C) **imagery** (D) repetition, (E) non sequiturs, and (F) pauses and silences, as well as the use of common words and the rhythms and patterns of everyday conversation.

Cliches

Pinter sprinkles **cliches** through his work, as though to give it a homey flavor, and they are usually related to the home and family or doing a good job-nice middle-class pronouncements. Occasionally, however, the very familiarity of the **cliche** gives it a whole new meaning because of its context. Lenny's two stories about his adventures with women, told to Ruth at their first meeting, are filled with cliches, but the subject of his talk is so different from the innocuously familiar **cliches** that they become startling. Ruth's final words to Teddy as he leaves to return to America are the epitome of the play, they sum up its entire meaning so aptly because they are a **cliche**. When Ruth calls, "Eddie. . . . Don't become a stranger," she is repeating an emotionless ritual used with casual acquaintances which seems shockingly inappropriate. But it is not, of course. The **cliche** sums up the emotion which is present, since there is very little. Ruth feels neither animosity nor love for this husband who has failed to satisfy her emotional requirements. He does not fulfill a function so she dismisses him, casually perhaps, perhaps even with some affection for their life together, but it is a dismissal which will never be overcome.

Jargon

Jargon also serves several purposes in Pinter's writing. The use of technical words is sometimes an attempt to cover an inability to communicate. In trying to find the right words to express a meaning, a character often hits upon a set of words which allow him to get sidetracked and therefore postpones his need to continue in the attempt to communicate, at least for a while. It works as a defense mechanism in much the same way.

Pinter has acknowledged that he gets "a considerable pleasure" from words (the delightful revue sketch "Trouble in the Works" is a classic example of his enthusiastic use of technical jargon). This may in part explain Lenny's familiarity with, and free use of, terms from the docks ("jibbing," "boom," "yardarm") and philosophy ("logical incoherence," "central affirmations of Christian theism"), though more importantly they tell the audience something about his character. When he talks about the girl with the "pox," whom he "clumped," and the old lady's "arse," the old lady whom he gave a "short-arm jab to the belly," he is speaking the language of the underworld of pimps and prostitutes. Verification: which is really Lenny's world? The fact that Ruth has no trouble following these terms indicates that she is as at home with them as he is.

The collective bargaining session at the end of the play where Ruth negotiates her contract is one of Pinter's "strategems to cover nakedness" that he talks about in "Between the Lines." "Installments," "original outlay," and "capital investment" all speak of a language locked beneath the language being used.

Finally, there is a combination of effects as in the discussion of philosophy. Often in Pinter the struggles for domination take the form of verbal battles, and Lenny is trying to beat his brother in his brother's own particular field. Ruth takes off from this point, though, to suggest that the words themselves are not important, that there is something which lies below them, just as there is a leg under her underwear. Perhaps the fact that lips move is more significant than the sounds which come through them. Jargon has led to this point and surely the reality which lies below the technical language is more important than the words which try to describe that reality.

Imagery

Imagery is a poetic device used to give writing life by appealing to the senses. In *The Homecoming* the images are certainly vivid and convey clear mental pictures. Significantly, most of the images deal with corruption. Max's descriptions of Jessie and himself have already been cited. In the same vein are Sam's description of Mac as a "lousy stinking rotten loudmouth. A bastard uncouth sodding runt," and Max's complaint that he is "lumbered" with "One cast-iron bunch of crap after another. One flow of stinking pus." It is hard to imagine passages which would have more emotional impact based on sensory involvement.

Repetition

Repetition is one of Pinter's most versatile linguistic devices. A typical pattern can be seen in the conversation between Lenny and Sam when Sam first enters in Act One:

> Lenny. How are you, Uncle?
>
> Sam. Not bad. A bit tired.
>
> Lenny. Tired? I bet you're tired. Where you been?
>
> Sam. I've been to London Airport.

Lenny. All the way up to London Airport? What, right up the M4?

Sam. Yes, all the way up there.

Lenny. ... Well, I think you're entitled to be tired, Uncle.

Sam. Well, it's the drivers.

Lenny. I know. That's what I'm talking about. I'm talking about the drivers.

Sam. Knocks you out.

Pause.

.... I took a Yankee out there today ... to the airport.

Lenny. Oh, a Yankee, was it?

Sam. Yes. ... I took him right thi way out to the airport.

Lenny. Had to catch a plane there, did he?

Sam. Yes.

Esslin notes that Pinter uses repetition in eight ways: (1) as a means of conveying dramatic information; (2) with characters who are struggling to find a specific word; (3) because of the enjoyment with the sound of that word once it has been found; (4) as a form of hysteria; (5) to indicate the process of absorbing a fact; (6) as a **refrain**; (a) to show preoccupation with an idea, or (b) as an assertion; (7) to indicate a lack of emotion, which can produce a train of associations; and (8) when a character is lying.

(1) Information can be imparted through repetition in several ways. When Max remembers knocking about with MacGregor, for instance, Max notes that MacGregor was called Mac and asks Lenny if he remembers Mac. Max goes on to say that Mac's whole family were MacGregors, but that he was the "only one" they called Mac, and then mentions that he was "very fond of your mother, Mac was." The constant use of the name Mac is telling the audience something not only about Mac, but also about the relationship between Mac and Max. Furthermore, it says something about the relationship between Max and Lenny. It is an attempt by this gruff old man to communicate with his son, and since he does not really know how to communicate, he repeats a word, a fact that he can be sure of-Mac.

(2) When characters in Pinter's plays find a word that they have been struggling to find, a word which suits their meaning perfectly, they use it over and over. Lenny is disgusted with Max's cooking, so he asks his father why he does not buy a dog; after all, he is a "dog cook," he thinks that he is "cooking for a lot of dogs."

(3) Having found a word they have been searching for, the characters often become enamored with its sound, reciting it almost ritualistically and in different combinations. Lenny's fixing on the word dog, cited above, is also related to this function of repetition.

(4) As a given individual becomes more emotionally upset, specific words echo through their conversation more and more frequently. There is a kind of hysteria in Teddy's preoccupation with the word "bed" when he and Ruth first enter the house. He

wants to see if his bed is still in his old room, even though he knows that everyone in the family has his own bed. He finds that his bed is still there, and after suggesting to Ruth that they go to bed, he becomes involved with the word "sheets." The words themselves are of little consequence, but Teddy's continual reference to these objects suggests his abstracted state of mind.

(5) Pinter uses repetition occasionally to indicate the process of absorbing a fact. When Lenny sees Ruth walk through his front door he rightly assumes that she must be connected with his brother, yet in spite of her explanation that she is his brother's wife, Lenny finds it difficult to understand the relationship. Pinter may be hinting that such definitions have no meaning; nonetheless, Lenny, after ignoring her answer comes back to the question later when he wonders if she lives with his brother, then finally, after another interruption in the train of thought, he comes to the conclusion that they must be newly-weds. It is a long process, but by constantly returning to his subject, Lenny has managed to grasp the concept.

(6) In a very poetic way, words continually reappear throughout a Pinter drama until they become a sort of **refrain** which builds to a cumulative effect which has a direct bearing on the meaning of the play. In *The Homecoming* there are several such words, among the most frequently repeated being "family" and words related to "home." Although these words appear naturally enough in the dialogue, they are what Pinter is concerning himself with in this play, and as an overall effect they serve as indicators subtly to keep attention fixed on the subject at hand - though the attention may be on an almost subconscious level.

(a) In the play the constant use of a word such as "family" until it becomes a running **refrain** indicates the preoccupation with the idea of a family by the characters who so incessantly find a way to employ the word in their conversation.

(b) Similarly, the characters, and in particular Max, manage to mention the word "mother" innumerable times during the course of the play. There seems to be a distinction between ordinary women and women who have become mothers. As an assertion, the stress placed on the word by its many repetitions implies that Ruth is acceptable to the men because she is a mother as Jessie was.

(7) Speeches which have no emotional impact for the speaker at times reflect the lack of emotion through the repetitions involved. Lenny's tall tales fit this pattern. The stories about girls making proposals, old ladies and their iron mangles, and trips to Venice have no emotional connection as a story, as far as Lenny is concerned, though they may demonstrate an underlying emotional basis. Consciously, however, he moves simply from idea to idea as each occurs to him through the process of association. If the stories held any real meaning for him, he would tell them in a straightforward manner. As it is, the fact that he moves according to imaginative whim proves the lack of importance the tales hold for him.

(8) In a like manner, a character who is lying tends to repeat himself, whether in trying to get the facts straight in his own mind as he creates them, or in trying to convince his listener purely by the weight of his repetitions (if someone keeps saying the same thing, it must be true). Joey's account of his adventure with the birds in the Scrubs is an excellent example of this use of repetition.

Non Sequiturs

A non sequitur is an inference which does not follow from the preceding premise. In ordinary conversation this generally takes the form of a statement or answer which is unrelated to the dialogue which went before, and suggests that the speaker either cannot or will not follow the train of thought being expressed in the conversation, or that the speaker is so preoccupied with his own thoughts that he has not heard what went before, or he must intrude his subject into the discussion whether it fits or not. In a play where the characters are avoiding communication and are completely involved with their personal worries they talk around, rather than at or to, one another. They may be talking about the same things, but they skirt around actually admitting their subject. Besides mirroring normal speech patterns, non sequiturs can be humorous and/ or convey information about their speakers. When Lenny moves from his story about the girl with the pox to talking about Ruth's marriage without any logical transition, all three operations are, in effect, one of the many examples in the drama in which this can be seen.

Pauses And Silences

Pinter's attention to pauses and silences is, along with repetition, his most distinctive linguistic element. The author has been able to joke about his use of this aspect of language-he has mentioned, for example that the reason that *The Caretaker* found a greater critical reception when it was first performed than did *The Birthday Party* is that critics are able to distinguish between when he uses dashes to indicate a pause and when he employs dots to accomplish the same end.

The importance of non-language is apparent to Pinter, too, as demonstrated by his statements in "Between the Lines." Realizing the relevance of Pinter's breaks in conversation, director Peter Hall is said to have held a "dot and pause" rehearsal, for the members of the original *The Homecoming* cast, which was "apparently very valuable," according to Pinter.

Pauses in the dialogue serve many purposes in *The Homecoming*, from actual lapses in the conversation to indications of extreme emotional involvement. However they are used, they tend to emphasize the subject matter. Ruth's description of her home in America is not long in actual word count, but the time it takes her to relate it is drawn out by the pauses between her statements, pauses which make America sound even more barren than her description of it would indicate because of the obvious emotional affect the sterility of her surroundings has imposed upon her. Since she is so profoundly affected that she can hardly utter her words, the sterility must be overpowering.

Esslin notes that there is a distinct difference intended when Pinter indicates a pause, as opposed to a silence. Pauses, Esslin contends, demonstrate that the thought process is continuing, and contribute to a developing of tension by exposing the intensity of the thought which has not yet broken into a verbally communicable pattern. Silences, on the other hand, serve to signal the conclusion of one line of thinking and the beginning of a new subject of conversation. The finest example of this practice comes when Lenny has finished telling Ruth about the girl with the pox and she wonders how he knew that the girl was diseased: How did I know?

Pause.

I decided she was.

Silence.

You and my brother are newly-weds, are you?

Pinter has managed to convey the importance of Lenny's answer through the use of a pause. And it is an important answer, related to the underlying theme of appearance versus reality, of the idea of verification. The pause tells the audience that Lenny is contemplating his answer, and it is not, therefore, likely to be what would normally be expected-if it has to be considered, it must be of some consequence.

The silence which follows Lenny's pronouncement is another signal for the audience, this time indicating that discussion on the topic of diseased girls is closed and a new topic is to be offered. The break is clear-cut and the audience is thus prepared to go on to something new.

THE HOMECOMING AND OTHER WORKS

THE COMEDIES OF MENACE

THE ROOM (1957)

The Room was first presented professionally at the Hampstead Theatre Club, January 21, 1960.

DRAMATIS PERSONAE

Bert Hudd - an inarticulate man of fifty.

Rose Hudd - Bert's wife, a frightened woman of sixty.

Mr. Kidd - a confused old man, landlord of the Hudds.

Tod Sands - a young man looking for a room to let.

Mrs. Clarissa Sands - Tod's wife.

Riley - a blind Negro who emerges from the basement seeking Rose.

Critical Analysis

Pinter's first play, *The Room*, contains nearly all of the elements (both thematic and stylistic) that he will develop through the first ten or twelve years of his playwriting career. The drama is typical in its exposure of menace by creating problems in verification and communication, using humor and realistic language as contrasting devices, and reliance on few, albeit extremely vivid, images. In other words, like the other "comedies of menace," much of the effectiveness of the play is due to the atmosphere of menace it exudes.

Meaning

In this play the dramatist is concerned primarily with exposing the existence of menace and then examining the individual, in this instance Rose, disintegrating under the pressure of that exposure.

Technique

The mood of menace is evoked, first of all, from the setting. There is a room, and there is a door into that room. From Rose's **imagery** it is clear that the room represents security to her-it is warm, it is the right size, it is isolated, "You've got a chance in a place like this." The presence of the door, on the other hand, implies a means of access for whatever is outside. It is also equally clear that what is outside is not good-it is dark, it is cold. What is worse, something from the small, dark, smelly, cold, moist basement might come through the door.

And it does. First Mr. Kidd heightens Rose's anxiety when she cannot communicate with him. She wants reassurance, but he only provides her with ambiguity. Next come the Sands with their knowledge that there is someone in the basement and the information that her room is to be let.

The actual violation of Rose's sanctuary comes in the form of a seemingly helpless, blind Negro, whose sole line of attack is to ask her to return home with him. At the play's conclusion Rose has been struck blind because of her exposure to the world outside her room. She has realized that she cannot be safe even in her own room and she has retreated as far as possible-into her skull.

Theme

Nowhere in *The Room* did the author indicate why Riley should be pursuing Rose, or why she fears him. The reason is not important. What is important is the realization that menace exists and that the individual is vulnerable to it.

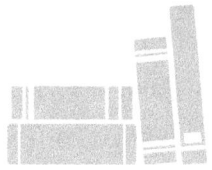

THE HOMECOMING AND OTHER WORKS

THE BIRTHDAY PARTY

The Birthday Party was first presented at the Arts Theatre, Cambridge, April 28, 1958.

DRAMATIS PERSONAE

Petey Boles - A man in his sixties who is a deck-chairs attendant at an English coastal resort.

Meg Boles - Petey's wife, a sloppy woman in her sixties who runs their boarding house.

Stanley - a man in his late thirties, an ex-pianist who is the only lodger staying at the Boles'.

Lulu - a neighbor girl in her twenties.

Nat (Simey) Goldberg - a Jew in his fifties who comes seeking Stanley.

Dermot (Seamus) McCann - a "recently unfrocked" Irish priest of thirty who is Goldberg's partner.

Critical Analysis

The Birthday Party continues the patterns initiated in *The Room*. The same techniques are brought to bear on the same themes, with a slight variation. The exposure of the existence of menace and its deteriorating effect on a character, expressed through lapses in communication and verification, are again the dramatist's primary focus.

Again the menace in *The Birthday Party* is unidentified and external, as it was in *The Room*. However, the reason for the existence of the menace being ambiguous does not lie in the absence of clues as in the previous play, but rather arises from the multitude of mutually contradictory sins and faux pas Goldberg and McCann accuse Stan of committing. Because of the nature of the attackers, it is implied that Stan, a sensitive man, has alienated himself from society and has to be broken so that he can fit into his niche once more.

Again, though, it is not important what crime Stan has committed-he has done something wrong, sometime in his life. Rose's "crime" is very personal because of its lack of definition. The possibilities expounded about what constitutes Stanley's crime are so broad that the feeling of menace extends to include the audience, since everyone has done something, sometime. We fear for Rose-Stan makes us aware that we should fear for ourselves.

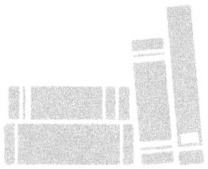

THE HOMECOMING AND OTHER WORKS

THE DUMB WAITER

The Dumb Waiter was first presented at the Hampstead Theatre Club, January 21, 1960, with *The Room*.

DRAMATIS PERSONAE

Ben - a quiet hired killer.

Gus - his questioning partner.

Critical Analysis: The third of the "comedies of menace," *The Dumb Waiter* marks the end of Pinter's first playwriting phase. It continues along the same lines as *The Room* and *The Birthday Party*, taking up where the latter leaves off. Ben and Gus are Goldberg and McCann seen from another perspective. Gus has begun questioning things as they are and the status quo of the organization (by implication, society), is threatened, so he must be removed. *The Dumb Waiter*, then, is a play in which the menacers are menaced.

THE HOMECOMING AND OTHER WORKS

A SLIGHT ACHE

A Slight Ache was commissioned to be broadcast on the British Broadcasting Corporation's Third Programme on July 29, 1959 and was subsequently staged for the first time at the Arts Theatre, London, January 18, 1961.

DRAMATIS PERSONAE

Edward - a middle-aged man who meets life unsuccessfully.

Flora - his unsatisfied wife.

Matchseller - the silent, filthy, ragged "menace" they invite into their house and christen Barnabas.

Critical Analysis: *A Slight Ache* is a transition play between the "comedies of menace" and the author's later dramas. It actually is a comedy of menace, with one significant difference - the menace is brought into The Room and it proves to be harmless. The real menace derives from the individual himself.

In the earlier days the menace was external and physical. In *A Slight Ache* it has become internal, psychological.

Pinter has started in a new direction with this drama, but he is still concerned with menace per se and its effects. Although the essence of the later plays is present, he does not exploit it as he will later when he concentrates on cause (as opposed to effect).

THE HOMECOMING AND OTHER WORKS

THE CARETAKER

....

The Caretaker was first presented at the Arts Theatre, London, April 27, 1960.

DRAMATIS PERSONAE

Mick - an enigmatic man in his late twenties who owns the house that his brother, Aston, is living in and who tries to protect Aston from outside threats.

Aston - the brother, a man in his early thirties who has undergone electric shock therapy.

Mac (Jenkins) Davies - an old man, invited into the house by Aston, whose intrusion threatens the relationship of the two brothers.

Critical Analysis: Asked what *The Caretaker* is about, Pinter has replied, "Love." A difficult play to interpret without this remark, with it *The Caretaker* assumes great importance in the dramatist's thematic evolution, for it indicates that he is consciously aware of the difference between this play and his earlier works. His emphasis has shifted from menace to the source of menace.

As for explaining *The Caretaker* in terms of love, it is obvious that if Davies is to be included. Pinter's definition of love cannot be the conventional dictionary definition that sees love as an unselfish devotion and "affection based on admiration or benevolence" in which the loved one is cherished for his intrinsic value. Aston, Mick, and Davies are all three involved in trying to form lasting personal relationships, and if this is what Pinter intends to convey by the word "love," perhaps we should substitute the word "need," which seems better suited to the relationships developed in the play.

Pinter has now become interested in what creates menace, and when he says that the drama concerns "love" (read "need") he allows a clearer understanding of the meaning of the piece, of what motivates the characters' actions. If Mick, Aston, and Davies all have some basic emotional and psychological needs and all of their actions are devoted to trying to fulfill those needs, the otherwise inexplicable series of confrontations in the play become understandable.

THE HOMECOMING AND OTHER WORKS

THE COLLECTION

The Collection was first presented by Associated-Rediffusion Television, London, on May 11, 1961 and staged at the Aldwych Theatre, London, June 18, 1962.

DRAMATIS PERSONAE

Harry Kane - a man in his forties, the owner of a posh house in Belgravia which he shares with Bill Lloyd.

James Home - a man in his thirties, Stella's husband; he works in dress designing.

Stella Home - James' wife, a woman in her thirties; she works with her husband.

Bill Lloyd - a man in his late twenties who shares Harry Kane's house; he, too, is engaged in dress designing.

Critical Analysis: While it is quite easy to see that *The Collection* is a dramatic **exposition** of one of Pinter's favorite themes, verification (and consequently the employment of one of his favorite devices, the continual juxtaposition of "true" but contradictory facts), the drama also fits into the emerging pattern of exploring individual psychological needs as a source of menace. This play really inaugurates the author's second major period of dramatic expression.

As in *The Caretaker*, the actions of all of the characters in *The Collection* are predicated on need. It is evident that the relationships between the two couples - Harry and Bill, and James and Stella - are not satisfactorily fulfilling certain needs in at least one member of each pairing. So they try to strengthen their bonds by showing that they can be broken and, therefore, require strengthening. In this play, then, Pinter has begun his exploration of how the menace of unfulfilled psychological needs creates actions aimed at finding satisfaction.

THE HOMECOMING AND OTHER WORKS

THE LOVER

The Lover first appeared on Associated-Rediffusion Television on March 28, 1963 and was first staged at the Arts Theatre, London, September 18, 1963, Harold Pinter directing.

DRAMATIS PERSONAE

Richard - the non-jealous husband who returns as Max, the lover.

Sarah - Richard's wife/mistress.

John - a milkman.

Critical Analysis: The **theme** of psychological need and the extent to which Pinter feels people will go in order to satisfy their sufficiencies is better seen in *The Lover* than in any of the dramatist's previous works. The obviousness of the **theme** results from the characters' being a little more desperate in their need to maintain or create a lasting relationship than characters presented heretofore, and their resulting actions are, therefore, a little more removed from the social norm. Consequently, we are more aware of what is happening and why it is happening.

THE HOMECOMING AND OTHER WORKS

OVERVIEW

Introduction

As was true with the major works, much of what appears in *The Homecoming* can be found in the author's minor plays. Basically, the difference between the major and minor pieces lies in the amount of time Pinter devoted to making his point. Necessarily, too, of course, the interrelationships of themes, the complexities of plot interaction, the more thorough characterization, and the diversity of techniques, all of which fold back on one another, reinforcing and underscoring, cannot be present in a short piece such as a two or three minute revue sketch to the degree that they are in the longer works. However, because all of Pinter's work is very much a single piece, examination of his lesser-known plays will also help contribute to our understanding of *The Homecoming*.

EXAMINATION OF THE MINOR WORKS

Kullus

Pinter's earliest known dramatic endeavor, Kullus dates from as early as 1949, according to John Russell Taylor. In this three-page sketch, Kullus is invited by the narrator into his room where the two exchange places. Before long there is an invitation to reverse the situation.

The Examination

The Examination, a monologue first published in 1959, relates the Examiner's interview with a character again named Kullus. During the course of the examination, Kullus gradually becomes the dominant figure, and by the end of the piece the roles of the two men have been reversed.

The Revue Sketches

The Revue Sketches are a series of ten short pieces generally to be included in Delsey Jones' musical revue *One to Another* or *Pieces of Eight*, both of which were produced in 1959. The pieces are commonly short and amusing.

"The Black and White" portrays a moment in the lives of two old women who apparently pass their evenings in milk bars watching all-night busses go by.

"Trouble in Works" brings management (Fibbs) and labor (Wills) together as Pinter has fun with language, using pseudo-mechanical jargon about products in a factory to demonstrate another failure in communication.

Pinter claims that the script of "Getting Acquainted," described as "a farcical **episode** built around a Civil Defense practice" by John Russell Taylor, has been lost.

"Special Offer" is a short selection in which a B.B.C. secretary is disturbed by a sale of men at a London firm.

"Last to Go" is an exercise in which a barman and an old newspaper seller talk at, instead of to, one another, each bouncing words off the wall that is the other, as they talk about which newspaper was the last to be sold on this particular night. Their responses are related to, though not necessarily relevant to, the words of the other, as they go through the motions of making conversation. The form is there, it is the meaning which is absent, and it is this incongruity which creates the humor.

The repetition of a ritual is essential in "Request Stop," too, but the lack of communication has taken on much more serious overtones.

In "Applicant," a physicist, Lamb, cheerfully enters an office to apply for a vacant post. A Miss Piffs subjects him to a little test to determine his psychological suitability. The test consists of asking the applicant a series of unrelated and usually irrelevant questions while he is attached to an electric apparatus of some sort which intermittently flashes bright lights or makes improbable noises.

The keynote to "Interview" is incongruity. Conducted in the form of an interview, the sketch considers the plight of the pornographic book trade at "Xmas" time. An insight into the workings of the human mind which can rationalize anything, the sketch proceeds in a manner typical of Pinter in that it is both humorous and horrifying at the same time when the bookseller reveals that he has determined that all of his customers are "Communists!"

"That's All" is another slice of life on the order of "The Black and White." Once again two women are presented discussing the everyday nature of their lives, revealing the monotony of their existence as they do so.

"That's Your Trouble" concerns an argument and the breakdown of meaningful communication between two strangers.

A NIGHT OUT (1960)

A Night Out continues the break from the comedy of menace pattern, as Pinter traces the attempts of Albert Stokes to break away from his mother's domination. As the title implies, the play is a departure from The Room motif, but the problems confronting the characters are the same - the need for communication between a mother and her son, and the need of lonely people for illusions.

THE DWARFS (1960)

Pinter's *The Dwarfs* is based on an unfinished autobiographical novel that he worked on between 1953 and 1957. It is commonly regarded as his most mystifying play. The questions of identity and verification compose the subject matter and the crux to understanding this admittedly obscure drama about Pete, Mark, and Len. As in *The Caretaker*, also written during this period, there has been a shift from the perspective of the early plays in which the audience wondered about who Rose, Riley, Stanley, or Goldberg and McCann were; the wondering has become internalized in these newer plays, and the characters themselves wonder who and what they are.

NIGHT SCHOOL (1960)

Although Pinter feels that *Night School* is one of the worst things he has ever written, it is not a bad play, and provides yet another source of material to be used in understanding his better pieces. Verification and the battle for a room are once more the subjects of Pinter's work as Wally must depose Sally, even though he may be losing his sole chance for salvation in doing so.

TEA PARTY (1963)

Pinter's first full family play, *Tea Party* records the disintegration of Robert Disson, head of one of the biggest sanitary equipment companies in England. Originally written for radio, then translated to television before becoming a stage play, *Tea Party* consists of a series of short scenes in which the **protagonist** finds himself unable to verify anything. Critics have not agreed about the meaning of this moody drama, but many of the familiar "Pinteresque" (a word Pinter is reportedly not fond of) elements reappear.

THE BASEMENT (1967)

The Basement, entitled *The Compartment* in its original version, is an extension of Pinter's earliest dramatic piece, Kullus. The ritualistic cycle of nature, relationships, love, communication, and security/insecurity are all explored in this interesting little play as Tim Law and Stott jockey roles while Jane looks on.

Three After-Pieces

The three short pieces which follow *The Homecoming* are Pinter's most inconsequential works since the review sketches, and they are not as amusing. In *Landscape* (1968) an old couple reminisces, possibly about their life together when they were young, but they never really talk about the same things as it is clear that they live lives separated by their personal perspectives. *Night* (1969) is a seven-minute sketch portraying a married couple likewise recalling their first meeting and early happiness in stories so divergent that they might be talking about unrelated events. *Silence* (1969) displays two men and a woman separately musing over their enigmatic triangular connection and the past. In these three plays, almost devoid of action, Pinter is concentrating on memory (partly as a function of verification) more than he has in the past, and this may prove to be a new direction in the continuing development of his work.

Summary

As can be seen from the preceding overview of Pinter's plays, there are fundamental concepts, themes, and techniques which are repeated throughout each of his plays. More importantly, the overview of his work shows that he is not merely rewriting the same drama over and over again. Rather, there is visible evidence of development taking place with every play presenting different aspects, new combinations, and varied perspectives of the artist's main concerns, all of which form a background as well as the material for *The Homecoming*.

THE HOMECOMING AND OTHER WORKS

SURVEY OF CRITICISM

Generally there are two criticisms which can be applied to commentaries on Pinter's work. First, his work is seldom seen as a piece, considered as a whole, each play viewed in relationship to the rest of his dramas. Similarities in plot and technique, relationships between characters, and occasional mentions of typical concepts have been cited, but very little has been done in the way of a systematic tracing from drama to drama of the themes which compose the core of the author's writing. Second, those thematic studies which are available are in the main either so superfluous as to lose meaning or so concentrated on a specific that they tend to invalidate themselves by ignoring a goodly portion of the play being examined. They do not go into enough detail about an entire play to take into account all the aspects of that one work. Conversely, perhaps because it is both easier and more obvious with less chance of misinterpretation, there has been a great deal written about the subject of Pinter's various dramatic techniques, in particular his uniquely effective handling of language, spoken and non-spoken.

Among those critics who have considered Pinter as an existentialist writer, John Pesta in "Pinter's Usurpers," *Drama Survey, VI* (Spring 1967), 54-65, finds that in Pinter's dramas there is typically a menacing "usurper" figure who undermines the existential security of those about him while his own existence is simultaneously being undermined. Walter Kerr's existential study of Pinter, *Harold Pinter*, No. 27 in the series "Columbia Essays on Modern Writers," New York and London, 1967, contests that the dramatist is alone among current writers in constructing plays in which the form reflects the existential **themes** of "existence precedes essence" and "man makes himself which are the subjects of those plays. Kerr writes that *The Homecoming*, which he feels is too long, is concerned with the problem of constantly changing identity. Ruth is seen as a catalytic agent who is continually shifting roles. Teddy is concerned with categories and may therefore be classified as a Platonist, the opposite of existentialist Ruth.

In the revised edition of *The Theatre of the Absurd*, New York, 1969, Martin Esslin combines an existential approach to Pinter's work with a Freudian interpretation. First he traces the extension of the **themes** of reality versus wish fulfillment found in *The Lover* as they appear in *The Homecoming*. The question of identity is again involved. He goes on, then, to interpret the play as a wish-fulfillment/dream sequence in which the sons seek the "sexual conquest of the mother and discomfort of the father." He also labels Ruth a "nymphomaniac," something for which there appears to be no basis in the play itself, and which, moreover, gives the drama an entirely new meaning-a meaning which cannot be supported by the evidence of the actions within the play. Pinter himself has explicitly denied that the woman can be considered a nymphomaniac. In *The Theatre of the Absurd*, Esslin spends little time on Pinter, as merely another of the authors who fit into this dramatic genre.

With *The Peopled Wound: The Work of Harold Pinter*, New York, 1970, however, Esslin has devoted an entire book to Pinter's writing. The sections on language and Pinter's outline-form biography are especially valuable. And in writing a whole book about only Pinter, Esslin has been able to extend his examination of *The Homecoming* to substantiate with details from the play some of the assertions he had made in *The Theatre of the Absurd*. He still traces an existential base, noting that Ruth is in a state of existential despair, but his emphasis in *The Peopled Wound* is on the combination of "a poetic image of the basic human situation" and Freudian symbology in which the "realistic action is a **metaphor** of human desires and aspirations, a myth, a dream image, a projection of archetypal fears and wishes." Esslin calls the play realistic because Pinter has provided only that information which would be available if the audience were actually witnessing these events taking place in a real house. The idea of dream images is contained in the theatrical portrayal of the Oedipal desires of the sons for their mother (replaced by Ruth in this case) and the humiliating rejection of their father.

In an earlier study, *Stratagems to Uncover Nakedness*, No. 6 in the "Missouri Literary Frontier Series," Columbia, 1969, Lois G. Gordon also symbolically interprets *The Homecoming* in Freudian terms, In this instance there is more a presumption that Pinter is presenting Freudian characters than there is a demonstration that this is so. Gordon admits that the artist is treating the "struggle for power and sexual mastery beneath the ritualized games of daily life," but goes on to comment on the "castrating, and castrated father" and then deals with the supposed homosexuality present. *Stratagems to Uncover Nakedness* is totally concerned with the sexual aspects of Pinter's drama.

Another reviewer who has commented on the homosexual content of *The Homecoming* is psychiatrist Abraham N. Franzblau, "A Psychiatrist Looks at *The Homecoming*," Saturday Review, 50:58, April 8, 1967. In his review of *The Homecoming* Franzblau states that the play is essentially the psychological stereotype of menage-a-trois, extended to include two additional men. The menage-a-trois is a homosexual situation in which two men make love to a common female companion, either in front of one another or at least with the knowledge of one another, deriving a homosexual satisfaction from the act. Franzblau contends that Pinter has created a "menage-a-cinq" in which Ruth will provide the four men involved with "heterosexual gratification" which in turn will produce "homosexual pleasure" as they share in one another's excitement.

Like Esslin, John Russel Taylor has published two studies of Pinter. The first, "A Room and Some Views," is a chapter in his longer examination of the British "Angry" theatre, *Anger and After*, revised edition, London, 1969 (published in New York under the title *The Angry Theatre*) and the second, No. 212 in Longman's "Writers and Their Work" series, Harold Pinter, London, 1969. In *Anger and After* Taylor neatly explains Pinter's technique for dramatizing his concept of verification. He also calls *The Homecoming* "a work of dazzling directness and simplicity" which is "about the battle between intellect and instinct, between thought and action." Teddy, and to some extent Sam, is the thinker in the family - and is paralyzed by his thought. The other men act, but it is Ruth who acts intuitively, who controls the play, and who eventually emerges victorious. Harold Pinter traces the development of the author's dramatic writing from the comedy-of-menace stage to the exploration of the questions of identity and the verifying of experience in his later pieces. Again Taylor asserts that *The Homecoming* is technically the "end-product" of all the author has learned in his playwrighting career. In his very short look at *The Homecoming*, Taylor concludes that memory is the controlling factor. Memory, "which is just the problem of verification seen from another angle," in some unexplained way or another debilitates all of the characters in the play with the exception of Ruth.

Arnold P. Hinchcliffe's *Harold Pinter*, No. 51 in "Twayne's English Authors Series," New York, 1967, is the earliest book-length study of Pinter. It is Hinchcliffe's opinion that *The Homecoming* "concerns the bonds that separate and unite what is conventionally a single unit," and that the play tests the morality which lies behind the concept of "the Family." Thus the drama reflects the attitudes of the characters to the status quo of the family situation. Hinchcliffe argues that since life is neither black nor white, the final judgment presented by the drama is not "unequivocal." He pictures Sam as pretending, and "probably" dying for, his belief in "goodness." Max and Joey are portrayed as having become "lost in the mess" [of life and the family and consequently not minding. Teddy, on the other hand, refuses to get lost in the mess-he rejects the status quo which he has tried to affect by his return but which has remained unchanged in spite of his efforts. Ruth, according to Hinchcliffe, has joined "the mess" to the extent that she can "beat the family at its own game." By default, then, Lenny becomes the "enigmatic center of the play, neither free nor lost; he is seeking, half in jest, to know what is the difference, what merits reverence, what is truth." Because of Ruth's demonstrated strength and Lenny's assumed character, Hinchcliffe regards the end of the play as possibly the beginning of the struggle which must ensue between these two characters who are now merely "measuring each other up."

Several other examinations of Pinter and *The Homecoming* are also useful. Bernard F. Dukore's "A Woman's Place," *Quarterly Journal of Speech*, LII (1967), 237-241, sees Ruth's role in *The*

Homecoming as a catalyst which brings out the animal instincts for a mating ritual among the members of the family. William J. Free discusses "Treatment of Character in Harold Pinter's *The Homecoming*" in the *South Atlantic Bulletin*, XXXIV, iv: 1-5. Kelly Morris' The Homecoming, *Tulane Drama Review*, XI (Winter, 1966), 185-191, sees the play as a sort of comedy of manners, in the tradition of Ibsen and Strindberg, combined with the aggressive nature of the family and a confusion of sexual roles.

John Lahr's interesting collection of critical essays and interviews, *Harold Pinter's* The Homecoming: *A Casebook*, New York, 1971, is the only book-length study devoted solely to treating *The Homecoming*. The casebook supplies few answers to the questions of motivation (indeed, there is disagreement between several of the authors), but it does furnish an excellent set of perspectives for approaching the work. Although there are defects, each selection does make valid observations and the result is a fuller understanding of the play, in part deriving from the interviews concerned with its first staging. These interviews are especially valuable, since the four men have reacted to the play, not tried to enforce interpretations upon it as the scholarly examinations sometimes do. Opening the book is an introduction "In Place of Biography" by Lahr which illustrates the concepts underlying the drama by providing a background which discusses the influence of Pinter's youth in Hackney. Martin Esslin's "*The Homecoming*: A Survey" restates his previous Pinter examinations, concluding that the piece is a "fantasy-dream of... sexual conquest" and insisting on Ruth's nymphomania. Director Peter Hall, in an interview conducted by Lahr, as are all the interviews, considers the problems of characterization, environment, and language faced in helping the cast perform in accordance with the play's meaning. In a second interview set designer John Bury explains how he tried to reflect Pinter's meaning in his set. Irving Wardel discusses "territorial struggle" as the drama's basic **theme** followed by Margaret Croyden's "Pinter's Hideous Comedy" which labels the play a combination of ritual, archetypes, and comedy of manners parody. "Pinter's Game of Happy Families" by John Russell Taylor restates some of the critic's excellent comments concerning the play's meaning and place in Pinter's canon. Steven M. L. Aronson's "Pinter's 'Family' and Blood Knowledge" deals with relationships between parents and offspring. Rolf Fjelde traces patterns found in the dramatist's plays. Bernard F. Dukore concentrates on Ruth's role, while Augusta Walker tries to answer why Ruth is willing to remain (to suffer more than life in America allows!). A second article of Lahr describes Pinter's language. This is followed by two additional interviews, the first a talk with John Normington about his portrayal of Sam in the original production. Involved is information about Pinter, rhythms of speech, Sam's role, and the Royal Shakespeare Company's interpretation of the drama. Paul Rogers, the original Max, similarly displays the insights developed by an actor coming to understand the character he portrays and its relationships to other characters. Finally, in "Pinter the Spaceman" (a third reprint - and needing some alteration for this particular collection), Lahr covers the subject of Pinter's naturalism. This last article originally appeared in *Evergreen Review*, No. 55 (June 1969) and again in Lahr's *Up Against the Fourth Wall*, New York, 1969, which is concerned with the modern theatre. Lahr has written on Pinter's naturalism in "Pinter and Chekhov: The Bond of Naturalism," *The Drama Review 13*, No. 2 (1968), 137-145.

In addition also helpful and interesting are the interviews with Pinter by Henry Hewes (an invaluable look at *The Homecoming* with comments by Pinter which are extremely important in understanding the play - "Probing Pinter's Play," *Saturday Review*, L, September 8, 1967, 56+) Lawrence M. Bensky (a highly informative and interesting interview in which Pinter talks about his background, writing career, influences on his writing, his concepts and techniques, and the writing process - "Harold Pinter, An Interview," *Paris Review*, X, 39, Fall, 1966, 12-37), and Kathleen Halton (an interview which includes useful background material and quotes by Pinter - "Pinter," *Vogue*, 150, October 1, 1967, 194-195+).

Other publications of interest are Lois Gordon's annotated bibliography (through mid-1967), "Pigeonholing Pinter: A Bibliography," *Theatre Documentation*, I, i, (1968) : 3-20; "Profile: Playwright on his Own," anon., *Observer* (September 15, 1963), 13, which includes an early biographical sketch; Harold Hobson's favorable reviews in *The Times* (London) which have announced Pinter's value from the first; and two Ph.D. dissertations, Patrick G. Conlon's Social Commentary in Contemporary Great Britain as Reflected in the Plays of John Osborne, Harold Pinter, and Arnold Wesker, Northwestern, 1969 and Steven H. Gale's Thematic Change in the Stage Plays of Harold Pinter, 1957-1967, University of Southern California, 1970.

Background material on Pinter, the Theatre of the Absurd, and contemporary British drama may be found in: Esslin's *The Theatre of the Absurd*; Taylor's *Anger and After*; William A. Armstrong (ed.), *Experimental Drama*, London, 1963; Eric Bentley, *The Playwright as Thinker*, Cleveland, 1955; Travis Bogard and William I. Oliver, *Modern Drama: Essays in Criticism*, New York, 1965; John R. Brown and Bernard Harris (eds.), *Contemporary Theatre*, Stratfordon-Avon Studies, No. 4, London, 1962; Robert Brustein, *The Theatre of Revolt*, New York, 1964 and *The Third Theatre*, New York, 1967; Albert Camus, *The Myth of Sisyphus*, Paris, 1942; Hazel Barnes, *The Literature of Possibility*, Lincoln, 1959; Joseph Chiarai, *Landmarks of Contemporary*

Drama, London, 1965; Esslin's *Absurd Drama*, London, 1965; Bamber Gascoigne, *Twentieth Century Drama*, London, 1962; David I. Grossvogel, *Four Playwrights and a Postscript*, Ithaca, 1962; Walter Kaufmann (ed.), *Existentialism from Dostoevsky to Sartre*, New York, 1956; Laurence Kitchin, *Mid-Century Drama*, London, 1960 and *Drama in the Sixties: Form and Interpretation*, London, 1966; John Mander, *The Writer and Commitment*, London, 1961; John Lahr, *Up Against the Fourth Wall*, New York, 1969; Charles Marowitz, Owen Hale, and Tom Milne, *The Encore Reader: A Chronicle of the New Drama*, London, 1965; Jean-Paul Sartre, *Being and Not-Being*, Paris, 1943; *Existentialism*, and *What is Literature*; J. C. Trewin, *Drama in Britain*, London, J. L. Styan, *The Dark Comedy: The Development of Modern Comic Tragedy*, Cambridge, 1962 and "The Published Play after 1956. II," *British Book News*, No. 301 (September, 1965), 601-605; Taylor, "British Drama of the 50s," *World Theatre*, XI (Autumn, 1964), 241-254; Ossia Trilling, "The New English Realism," *Tulane Drama Review*, VII (Winter, 1962), 184-193, and "The Young British Drama," *Modern Drama*, III (May, 1960), 168; Kenneth Tynan, *Tynan on Theatre*, London, 1964, and *Left and Right*, London, 1967; George E. Wellwarth, *The Theatre of Protest and Paradox*, New York, 1964; Raymond Williams, *Drama from Ibsen to Brecht*, London, 1968.

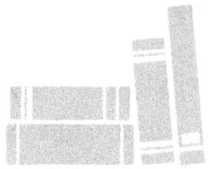

THE HOMECOMING AND OTHER WORKS

ESSAY QUESTIONS AND MODEL ANSWERS

The following essay questions and model answers are intended to suggest various approaches to understanding the meaning and techniques to be found in Pinter's *The Homecoming*, to help relate different aspects of the work to one another, to provide a means of review, and to indicate subjects for further research and discussion.

Question: Can Pinter legitimately be classified as a dramatist in the "Theatre of the Absurd"?

Answer: The answer to this question depends on several things, though many critics have considered Pinter an absurdist. First one must determine the definition of "Theatre of the Absurd," then examine the author's plays in the light of that definition (some of his dramas may fit the definition, while others obviously do not).

The concept of the "Theatre of the Absurd" grew out of Albert Camus' *The Myth of Sisyphus*, published in 1942, and was explicitly stated in *The Theatre of the Absurd* by Martin Esslin in his seminal study of this **genre** of the theatre in 1961. Camus feels that modern man has been cut off from the certitudes and basic assumptions of the past. Since faith in religion, progress, nationalism, democracy, and so forth have been destroyed by such events as the two world wars, he asserts that life has become meaningless (and calmly wonders why suicide should not be sought as an escape). As a result, man feels like a stranger in the universe-because he has been deprived of the intimisms of his past, he lacks the hope of his future: "This divorce between man and his life . . . constitutes the feeling of Absurdity."

Ionesco, in an essay on Kafka (1957), continues this line of thought when he defines the Absurd as that which is "devoid of purpose." The lack of purpose, the fact that all man's actions have become "senseless, absurd, useless," derives from the fact that man has lost his "religious, **metaphysical** and transcendental roots."

Esslin points out that "absurd" is defined as "out of harmony with reason or propriety; incongruous, unreasonable, illogical" and that it may also simply mean "ridiculous." In its application to the plays of Beckett, Ionesco, Adamov, Genet, Albee, Arrabal, Grass, Simpson, Pinter, and others, however, the term has come to mean not only an expression of the **theme** of the senselessness of the human condition, the **metaphysical** anguish at the absurdity of human life (the representative contemporary attitude of angst), but at the same time the form of its expression.

Thus Absurd dramas may lack plot, development, characterization, and common sense. In order to demonstrate the inadequacy of a logical, rational approach to life (which is neither logical nor rational), Absurd playwrights have ceased arguing about the absurdity of the human condition; instead they quite simply present life as they perceive it, with all its absurdities and contradictions.

One of the devices used by Absurdists to present their view of the world is the essentially anti-literary technique of devaluing language. What happens on the stage, therefore, often contradicts what the characters say is happening.

Some of Pinter's early dramas, then, might seemingly fit this pattern, when viewed in isolation. But when seen in the overall context of his total artistic output, it can be seen that these plays only partly realize the Absurd definition, because of the **themes** which can be traced through them. More importantly, *The Homecoming* is really definitely outside the "Theatre of the Absurd" tradition.

It is true that Pinter's work implies a world of angst caused by a lack of faith in religion, progress, or whatever. But it is only implied because Pinter does not concern himself with these matters. Perhaps such a world does underlie Pinter's theatre, perhaps this is the reason his characters seem cut off from more conventional concerns and apparently exist in rooms which have no bearing on the outside world of religion, or progress. Pinter's world does have meaning, however. In *The Homecoming* the characters are involved with something more basic than progress - they are involved with survival. The meaning of the play lies in the relationships the individuals are trying to create between each other, and the survival of their mental well-being is dependent upon how well they maintain these relationships. In the final analysis, then, the supposedly senseless actions portrayed on the stage are anything but illogical; they are undertaken as attempts to establish those relationships because life does have meaning, meaning contained in the relationships themselves.

Pinter's work only seems "Absurd" because he has cut through the superficial interests of the world. His focus is much deeper. It is on the essential components of human life itself. There can be no concern with such inconsequentials as nationalism until one has solved the problems of personal existence - and as the actions of all of Pinter's characters demonstrate, life does have meaning on this most basic level.

Question: Might Pinter be considered an "existentialist"?

Answer: This question is even harder to answer than that above, because of the numerous definitions of what constitutes existentialism, though many critics have labeled Pinter's writing as existential.

According to the Platonic concept of the universe, the visible world derives its reality from an invisible world of Forms and Ideas. This means, for example, that all chairs are based on, are representations of, a single perfect model of a chair, something which contains the essence of all chaimess. Man can be considered in the same way, and all men, in effect, are derived from the same pattern. This sets certain prescribed limitations on man, naturally, since all men must conform to specific parameters regarding their physical, mental, and moral capacities. It also means that man has an identity and can be secure in the knowledge that there is a logic of predetermined rules in the universe which must be followed. As an illustration of the principle of the invisible/visible worlds, the example of shadows on the wall of a cave has been advanced. We see the shadows, the representations of the ideal in the visible, "real" world in which we live. Aristotle posited the location of the perfect source of, which the shadows are mere representations, in the mind of God.

Existentialism asserts the contrary of a Platonic universe. To a large extent existentialism denies the existence of God, though there are "Christian existentialists," and the consequent pre-existence of Forms. Since World War II especially, existentialists like Jean-Paul Sartre have drawn a picture of a world in which insecurity, loneliness, and the irrevocability of man's experience are stressed. Because there are no fixed models, man is free and his future is undetermined, but this precludes the comfort and security of fixed values. Life becomes a series of choices.

Because there is no archetype of man in the universe, each man determines what he will be. His choices create himself. As Sartre says, "man makes himself - every action we undertake changes us in some way, makes us different from what we just were, but we have chosen to undertake that action, even if the choice involves not acting.

In relation to this idea that we are our own creations, that "the Child is father of the Man" in Wordsworth's words, Sartre insists that "existence precedes essence." Platonists agree that everything in the visible world descends from an essence which preceded its existence. Existentialists deny the archetype and argue that an individual must be aware of his existence before he can begin the process of determining his own essence.

Clearly there are elements of existentialism in Pinter's work. *The Dwarfs* contains innumerable fine examples of existential philosophy in the dialogue, yet there is no Pinter play which does not advance existential ideas to some extent. The loneliness, the insecurity, the constant search for personal identity are all existential in nature. Whether or not this defines Pinter as part of the Existential theatre, however, is something else.

Esslin states that the difference between the Theatre of the Absurd and the Existential theatre is that the Theatre of the Absurd strives to integrate its subject matter and the form in which that subject matter is expressed, while the Existential theatre attempts no such integration. He would say, in that case, that Pinter clearly does not belong to the Existential theatre movement.

Kerr holds the exact opposite opinion. He feels that Pinter is the only contemporary playwright who designs his plays so that they will function "according to [the] existentialist principle." He holds that sequence is of extreme importance and that concepts are inconsequential. For instance, existentialism pictures man as living in a void, yet **refrains** from conceptualizing this void. *The Room* certainly illustrates this principle. *The Homecoming* may not.

In examining *The Homecoming* Kerr notes that, if plays are written to reveal the "existence precedes essence" sequence, no character can be essentially anything. There can be no assigned role on the order of mistress, whore, or wife. He points out that characteristics of each individual must be constantly changing and that one must become for the moment what his actions are.

Kerr similarly assumes that, since Edward and Flora in *A Slight Ache*, Pinter's men are categorists while his women remain flexible, adjusting to any change and remaining undisturbed by the lack of categories. The woman becomes a catalyst, full of "shifting possibilities," who calmly moves from role to role Questions of identity do not concern her for she is continually in the process of "becoming."

Ruth in *The Homecoming* exhibits this same quality of being able to shift identity at will and with no adverse mental reactions. Kerr calls her the "center of the play" because of this "existential suppleness." The result of Pinter's having welded existential thought to the form of his plays, Kerr maintains, is a successful construction of a "series of felt realities that do not depend upon conceptual underpinning," which constitutes Kerr's definition of existential.

Question: How does *The Homecoming* fit into Pinter's overall thematic development?

Answer: The three basic concepts of menace, verification, and communication are present, but this being one of his later dramas, these **themes** are not part of his concern with exposing the existence of menace and its effect on the individual, but rather they are used to demonstrate individual psychological needs among his characters and their desperate attempts to satisfy those needs.

Question: What is *The Homecoming* "about"?

Answer: As reported above, Pinter has claimed that the play is "about love and lack of love," about people who "aren't acting arbitrarily but for very deep-seated reasons."

When viewed in the context of individual psychological needs, this statement means that each person in the drama is trying to form some sort of relationship with the other characters in the play in order to fulfill their emotional requirements (see especially the section on "**Character Analysis**" above).

Question: In what ways is the play realistic?

Answer: On a superficial level the language and paralanguage of the characters' dialogues is realistic, even superrealistic.

On the level of what Pinter is trying to say in this play, it is also realistic, though the actions do not seem to be so. Taking into account the desperation of the characters (see Question 5), the actions which take place are realistic and even logical attempts to achieve organistic homeostasis.

Pinter has mentioned that the family does behave fairly ruthlessly toward one another, "But they do it out of the texture of their lives" for reasons which are "desperate."

Question: Are Teddy's reactions to his wife's seduction realistic? Are they believable?

Answer: Pinter has logically answered this question by asking what would have happened if Teddy had interfered. It could only have led to a fight, and this particular man would do anything to avoid becoming emotionally involved. He has, after all, consciously divorced himself from such a vulnerable position or attitude. Besides, his history of failure and his demonstrated lack of control over his wife both indicate that he would serve no constructive purpose by interfering - they would ignore him, or kick him out. In addition, if Ruth is not meeting Teddy's requirements, he has no longer any need for her and can dismiss her from his interest. He is not involved with her emotionally, he is ineffective anyway-why bother protesting?

Question: How credible is it that Ruth would be willing to stay behind and become a prostitute?

Answer: Again, the **theme** of "love and lack of love" must be cited. Pinter, perhaps facetiously, has argued that such things occur constantly, because there are many women who are equally unsatisfied. More persuasively he tells us that it would not have happened if she had been happily married, but since her marriage was unsatisfying, there was no reason for her to confine herself to its limitations. The difference between Ruth's description of her life in America (sterile, bare, rocky) and her husband's glowing account shows her lack of satisfaction.

The dramatist also reminds us that there is no indication at the end of the play that Ruth is actually going to go off to Greek Street to engage in prostitution. Whether or not she will be up to her, for she has proven her domination over all the other characters in the play. Pinter additionally suggests that if she does decide to be a "prostitute," she will not be a prostitute in her own mind since she will be doing it not for money or sexual pleasure, but as a positive action in her continued attempt to find emotional fulfillment, whatever the source of that fulfillment.

Question: Why do the family members react as they do when Sam tells of Jessie's indiscretion with MacGregor? Why are they unshocked by his revelation and why are they unconcerned about his collapse?

Answer: There are some indications that at least some of the men were already aware of Jessie's activities, so would not be shocked. Whether they were previously aware or not does not really matter, though, for they are all too involved with their own personal problems to be concerned about someone else. Jessie, now that Ruth is replacing her, is no longer needed for their emotional balance and they can dispense with her as easily as Teddy abandoned Ruth.

The same thing is true in regard to Sam's collapse. It has no bearing on them. He is their concern only in relation to the amount of effect he has on their mental well-being, and if he has ceased to function in a satisfactory way, he is no longer worthy of their notice.

Question: Why does Teddy refuse to discuss philosophy with his brother?

Answer: Teddy's reluctance to engage in a philosophical disquisition with Lenny is symptomatic of his entire attitude toward life and relationships with other human beings.

Throughout his life Teddy has shown a consistent tendency toward failure. If he allows Lenny to engage him in a philosophical dispute, he would run the chance of being defeated-a double defeat since it would be in his own chosen field.

There is also the idea of domination involved. Verbal battles are a means of establishing domination in all of Pinter's works, and as Teddy has no reason to believe that he can defeat his younger brother, he does not want to enter into the struggle.

Finally, these two reasons form a third, all-encompassing reason-Teddy's relationships with other human beings. Because of his failures in the past, his demonstrated inability to understand or dominate his own wife, Teddy has retreated into nonidentification in order to protect himself from further failure experiences. He has created a defense mechanism by holding himself aloof.

Question: Compare Ruth's position in the family at the end of the drama with that of Jessie when she was alive.

Answer: Ruth's position as the play ends is quite similar to the position Jessie maintained in the family before her death, and in part it is Jessie's previous ubiquitous domination of the affairs of her husband, sons, and brother-in-law which allows Ruth to replace her with a minimum of effort. The men are used to a woman influencing every aspect of their lives and quickly adapt to the new situation when Ruth seems ready and willing (and able) to function as Jessie did.

That Ruth is the dominant character in the drama, there can be no doubt-she convincingly demonstrates her superiority over each member of the group in a careful, step-by-step manner. Once she has asserted her authority (and coincidentally her willingness and ability to supplant Jessie in all her roles), the men accept her according to their need, and she responds to each of them accordingly. For Joey she is a mother; for Max she takes over the responsibility of a wife; for Sam she is unattainable because she is another man's wife; for Lenny she is a woman to be respected and at the same time she is contemptible-he does not have to worry about her embarrassing him sexually, either.

Question: Why and how do the characters try to dominate one another?

Answer: The attempts at domination take many forms, but foremost are verbal battles, outright ridicule, complete ignoring of the "opponent," and calling basic assumptions into question.

The reason for the power struggle is never made clear by Pinter. It may be a part of human nature, it may be a means of fulfilling a psychological need, it may be an attempt at communication. It is also probably an attempt to satisfy the personal demand for verification-if a situation can be made to occur in which someone is dominant and someone else is placed in an inferior position, then the world has been ordered and made stable to some extent. Domination similarly works as a tool in establishing identity.

Pinter has admitted that "the question of dominance and subservience" is a repeated **theme** in his plays, and in talking with Bensky about "The Examination," a piece explicitly about a "battle for positions," he indicates that his interest is in the question of "who was dominant at what point... how they were going to be dominant... what tools they would use to achieve dominance... how they would try to undermine the other." He feels that there is a constantly present threat, a "very common, everyday thing," that has to do "with this question of being in the uppermost position, or attempting to be."

Question: What justification is there for regarding Ruth as a nymphomaniac?

Answer: Pinter has explicitly answered the question of Ruth's possible nymphomaniacal tendencies in speaking with Kathleen Halton, incidentally expressing the thematic interpretation of *The Homecoming* as a dramatic examination of the desperate actions involved in attempting to meet individual psychological requirements, which nullifies anything that does not aid in fulfilling those needs: "The woman is not a nymphomaniac as some critics have claimed. . . . She's in a kind of despair which gives her a kind of freedom. Certain facts like marriage and the family for this woman have clearly ceased to have any meaning."

For those critics who insist on calling Ruth a nymphomaniac, it should be pointed out that at no time in the drama is there any evidence that she actually makes love with anyone, let alone more than one of the men. She and Joey do not "go all the way," and the only other man she is in bed with is her husband - and they did not necessarily make love, since they went to bed at different times.

Question: Why does Pinter bring up the suggestion of prostitution?

Answer: The answer to this question is related to the answer to Question 12. Shock and contrast are both used by the dramatist in order to emphasize his point. Ruth is introduced as a seemingly normal woman-married, a housewife and mother. By suggesting that she is willing to accept a life of prostitution he has presented the opposite extreme of the normal world of the housewife and thus indicated the intensity of Ruth's desperation and the extent to which she has been driven in her attempts to satisfy her emotional demands.

Question: Discuss the **theme** of success in *The Homecoming*.

Answer: In Pinter the **theme** of success is really the theme of non-success. His characters are generally failures in almost every aspect of their lives.

Teddy's inability to control his wife or to achieve the purpose for which he returned home, as well as his probable history of unsuccessful relationships with other people, have combined to turn him into an automaton in an attempt to protect himself from further involvement which will undoubtedly only lead to further lack of success.

Sam failed his brother as a chaperone for Jessie, who committed adultery while he watched. He failed to keep Jessie's name unsullied, and he ultimately fails himself when his interruption of the proceedings of installing Ruth as the new mistress of the house does not halt her installation.

Mac has managed to hold his family together, but has alienated himself in doing so. He was outwitted by crooks before and now he is outwitted by his daughter-in-law.

Joey cannot force his lovemaking to a **climax**. As a boxer he has only two things to learn; how to defend himself and how to attack.

Lenny's tales of prodigious conquests over women are too Walter Mittyish to be taken literally. His initial meeting with Ruth demonstrates his incompetence, and his need to experience sensations vicariously through Joey strengthens the image of his futility. Nothing in the drama serves to reverse this picture of Lenny-he is easily defeated by Ruth and his sole successes come at the expense of Teddy, who will not enter into combat with him.

Ruth is the one character in the play who does exhibit a propensity for success. But it should be remembered that she has not succeeded in her marriage (and presumably her modeling career, otherwise she would not have abandoned it); and when the curtain comes down she has attained a position of power, though there is no way of knowing whether or not she will be able to maintain it, or if it really is the answer to what she is seeking.

Question: How can *The Homecoming* possibly relate to "real" life?

Answer: Speaking somewhat facetiously, Pinter has said that there is nothing out of the ordinary about women rolling off couches with "brothers, cousins, or next-door neighbors," for such an activity is purely a stark symptom of the desperation felt by these women.

Speaking less suggestively and more specifically, we can say that *The Homecoming* relates to "real" life in many provocative ways. It dramatizes the problems of communicating in a world of ambiguity, subjectivity, and doubt. It underscores the tragic tendency of the family to lapse into cannibalism, to foster sick conflict rather than healthy collaboration, to stultify the individual. It demonstrates how even well-educated persons can develop so-called "defense mechanisms" that become self-defeating. All in all, *The Homecoming* is a sober reminder that while trying to boomerang himself beyond Venus into Far Outer Space, man still has not developed the reliable power to love in his own primal groups.

Question: How does *The Homecoming* relate to your life? Can you apply what you have learned about human nature to your own behavior or to the behavior of those about you?

ANNOTATED BIBLIOGRAPHY

Alligaier, Dieter. Die Dramen Harold Pinter, Eine Untersuchung von Form und Inhalt (dissertation), Frankfurt, 1967, in German.

Amend, V. E. "Harold Pinter: Some Credits and Debits," Modern Drama (Summer, 1967), 10:165.

Ashworth, Arthur. "New Theatre: Ionesco, Beckett, Pinter," Southerly, XXII (1962), 145-152.

Discussion of Pinter as a Kafkaesque compromise between the Theatre of the Absurd and realistic theatre in that his characters and situations are realistic but become "twisted askew" during the course of their confrontations.

Bensky, Lawrence M. "Harold Pinter, An Interview," Paris Review, X (Fall, 1966), 39, 12-37.

A highly informative and interesting interview in which Pinter talks about his background, writing career, influences on his writing, his concepts and techniques, and the writing process.

____. "Pinter: Violence is Natural," New York Times, II (January 1, 1967), 1:7.

An interview about dramatic techniques.

Bernhard, F. J. "Beyond **Realism** The Plays of Harold Pinter," Modern Drama, VIII (September, 1964), 185-191.

The poetic quality of Pinter's language is examined and the techniques which make it superrealistic.

Brine, Adrian. "In Search of a Hero," Spectator, CCXI (February 26, (1965), 386.

Because of the functional non-functioning of dialogue in Pinter's plays, a new type of actor is needed to fulfill the demands of the roles.

____. "The Guilty Seam," Spectator, CCIV (January 29, 1960), 138.

Somewhere between Brecht and Chayevsky, Pinter's dramas of ritualism and manipulation remain "obstinately a-plicit (as opposed to 'explicit')."

Brown, John Russell. "Dialogue in Pinter and Others," Critical Quarterly, VII (Autumn, 1965), 225-243.

Pinter's dialogue, influenced by Beckett and Checkhov, lies behind his success. A study of the texture of that dialogue.

____. "Mr. Pinter's Shakespeare," Critical Quarterly, V (Autumn, 1963), 251-265.

With Beckett, Ionesco, and Shakespeare, Pinter shares the slow exposure of character and motivation through seemingly meaningless repetitions, silences, insistences, and denials which imply the underlying context of the character's actions. See also Bert O. States (below).

Brown, John Russell and Harris, Bernard (editors). Contemporary Theater, Stratford-on-Avon Studies, No.4, London, 1962.

Nine essays, including Leech's comparison of Pinter and Wesker.

Brustein, Robert. *The Theater of Revolt: An Approach to the Modern Drama*, Boston, 1962; London, 1965.

A study of rebellion in the theatre in existential terms; Pinter's debt to Pirandello is cited.

____. The Third Theatre, New York, 1970.

In his section on "The Thoughts from Abroad" Brustein says he does not like *The Homecoming*, which he clearly did not understand.

Bryden, R. "A Stink of Pinter," The New Statesman and Nation, LXIX (June 11, 1965), 928.

About Pinter's imagery.

____. "Pinter," The Observer, London (February 19, 1967).

Cohen, Mark. "The Plays of Harold Pinter," Jewish Quarterly, VII (Summer, 1961), 21-22.

Pinter's cliche-filled repetitious dialogue and **themes** of domination, menace, security, and the malignant organization are mentioned.

Cohn, Ruby. "Latter Day Pinter," Drama Survey, III (Winter, 1964), 366-377.

Pinter's career to this point displays a concern with appearance vs. reality, but it also shows technical progress.

____. "The Absurdly Absurd: Avatars of Godot," Comparative Literature Studies, II (1965), 233-240.

As examples of the Absurd, both Waiting for Godot and *The Dumb Waiter* exemplify the Absurd doctrine of man's awareness of his place in the universe thought the absurdity of the play's form.

____. "The World of Harold Pinter," Tulane Drama Review, VI (March, 1962), 55-68.

"Man vs. the System" with a "central victim-villain" conflict is proposed as Pinter's main **theme** as revealed through the cumulative use of symbols and dialogue.

Conlon, Patrick G. Social Commentary in Contemporary Great Britain as Reflected in the Plays of John Osborne, Harold Pinter, and Arnold Wesker (dissertation), Northwestern, 1969.

Craig, H. A. L. "Poetry in the Theatre," New Statesman, LX (November 12, 1960), 734, 736.

A discussion about the lack of verse drama in the contemporary theatre which comes to the conclusion that Pinter is one of the few artists who can still create a "mod, a pervasion of poetry."

Crist, Judith. "A Mystery: Pinter on Pinter," Look, XXXII, 26 (December 24, 1968), 77.

Dick, Kay. "Mr. Pinter and the Fearful Matter," Texas Quarterly, IV (1961), 257-265.

Stresses Pinter's concern with communication.

Drake, Carol Dixon. Harold Pinter and the Problem of Verification (thesis), University of Southern California, 1964.

A short study of Pinter's concept of verification (as delineated in the Royal Court program notes for the performance of *The Room* and *The Dumb Waiter*) as expressed in his dramas to this date.

Dukore, Bernard F. "A Woman's Place," Quarterly Journal of Speech, LII (1967), 237-241.

Ruth's role in *The Homecoming* is described as a catalyst which brings out the animal instincts for a mating ritual among the members of the family.

____. "Theater of Harold Pinter," Tulane Drama Review, VI (March, 1962), 43-54.

Pinter's theatre is seen as "a picture of contemporary man beaten down by the social forces around him," partly based on "man's failure to communicate with other men."

Esslin, Martin. Absurd Drama, London, 1965.

Discusses Pinter's plays and techniques on an individual basis and places the dramatist in the tradition of the Theatre of the Absurd.

____. "Harold Pinter, un dramaturge anglais de l'absurde," Preuves, No. 151 (1964), 45-54, in French.

____. "Godot and His Children: The Theater of Samuel Beckett and Harold Pinter," Experimental Drama, ed. William A. Armstrong, London (1963), 128-146.

Compares Beckett and Pinter, especially in the area of language which he finds most realistic in the latter. Decides that Pinter does not belong to the "kitchen-sink" school of dramatists in his almost allegorical presentation of the human condition.

_____. Harold Pinter, No. 38 in the series "Friedrichs Dramatiker des Welttheaters," Velber bei Hannover, 1967, in German.

_____. "Pinter and the Absurd," Twentieth Century, CLXIX (February 1961), 176-185.

Pinter's poetic use of dialogue is the factor which successfully creates an Absurd realism.

_____. "Pinter Translated," Encounter (March, 1968).

_____. The Peopled Wound: The Work of Harold Pinter, New York, 1970.

Information (some from Pinter) and background material not available elsewhere makes this book both interesting and important, although the mixture of psychological and existential interpretations of the plays is not always satisfactory. Contains an excellent section on Pinter's use of language and silence.

_____. The Theatre of the Absurd, 1965, revised edition, London, 1968; New York 1969.

Summarizes plays and deals with **themes** (menace) and techniques in general

Feynman, Alberta E. "The Fetal Quality of 'Character' in Plays of the Absurd," Modern Drama, IX (May, 1965), 18-25.

The characters in Pinter's plays are considered too nebulous to be true characters.

Fitzgerald, Marion. "Playwriting Is Agony, Says Hugh Leonard," Irish Digest, LXXIX (January, 1964), 34-36.

Leonard approves highly of Pinter as a playwright.

Franzblau, Abraham N. "A Psychiatrist Looks at *The Homecoming*," Saturday Review, L (September 8, 1967), 58.

A psychological interpretation of *The Homecoming* (as menage-a-trois) which does not seem to be based on either the characters or the action of the drama.

Free, William J. "Treatment of Character in Harold Pinter's *The Homecoming*," South Atlantic Bulletin, XXXIV, iv:1-5.

Frisch, Jack E. "Ironic Theater: Techniques of **Irony** in the Plays of Samuel Beckett, Eugene Ionesco, Harold Pinter and Jean Genet" (dissertation), University of Wisconsin, 1965.

Irony in the modern theatre is directed at the audience.

Gale, Steven Hershel. Thematic Change in the Stage Plays of Harold Pinter, 1957-1967 (dissertation), University of Southern California, 1970.

A study tracing the movement from the simple exposure of the existence of menace and its disintegrating effect on the individual in the "comedies of menace" to the later plays which examine the source of menace (individual psychological needs) and the desperate attempts of the characters to fulfill their needs.

Gascoigne, Bamber. "Cult of Personality," Spectator, CCVIII (June 29, 1962), 859.

Strindberg's influence on Pinter is considered.

Giannetti, Louis D. The Drama of the Welfare State (dissertation), University of Iowa, 1967.

Glover, William. "Pinter's Plays Reflect His Cool," Los Angeles Times (May 14, 1967).

Comments by Pinter about various plays included.

Gordon, Lois G. Harold Pinter, Columbia, Missouri, 1968.

Role playing, sex, etc. in Pinter's work are viewed from a Freudian viewpoint.

____. "Pigeonholing Pinter: A Bibliography," Theatre Documentation, I (1968), i:3-20.

A fairly thorough annotated bibliography through mid-1967.

Gray, Wallace. "The Uses of Incongruity," Commonweal, XV (December, 1963), 343-347.

Characteristic of the Absurdists, Pinter utilizes the three kinds of incongruity ("rational and meaningful, irrational and meaningless, and irrational and apparently meaningless") to develop both the meaning and humor in his plays.

Gross, John. " Amazing Reductions," Encounter, XXIII (September, 1964), 50-52.

Pinter's poetic drama is revitalizing the English theatre.

Guernsey, Otis L., Jr. The Best Plays of 1966-1967, New York, 1967.

Pinter's plays on Broadway.

Habicht, Werner. "Der Dialog und das Schweigen im 'Theater des Absurden," Die Neueren Sprachen (1967), in German.

Hafley, James. "The Human Image in Contemporary Art," Kerygma, III (Summer, 1963), 23-24.

Comparison of **themes** in the Theatre of the Absurd and Abstract Expressionism in art.

Halton, Kathleen. "Pinter," Vogue, 150 (October 1, 1967), 194-195+.

Includes useful background material and quotes by Pinter.

Hayman, Ronald, Harold Pinter, in the series" Contemporary Playwrights," London, 1968.

Hays, H.R. "Transcending Naturalism," Modem Drama, IV (May, 1962), 27-36.

The **realism** of Pinter's work covers the chaos which exists underneath.

Henry, Patrick. "Acting the Absurd," Drama Critique, VI (Winter, 1963), 9-19.

The actor's approach to performing a piece by Pinter.

Hewes, Henry, "Probing Pinter's Play," Saturday Review, L (September 8, 1967), 56+.

An invaluable look at *The Homecoming* with comments by Pinter which are extremely important in understanding the play.

Hinchcliffe, Arnold P. Harold Pinter, "Twayne's English Authors Series," New York, 1967.

Traces Pinter's development, concentrating on meaning of individual plays and the use of language. Although there are some holes, it is the most complete study prior to Esslin's.

____. "Mr. Pinter's Belinda," Modern Drama (September, 1968).

Hoefer, Jacqueline. "Pinter and Whiting: Two Attitudes towards the Alienated Artist," Modern Drama, IV (February, 1962), 402-408.

A comparison of *The Birthday Party* and Whiting's *Saint's Day* which examines the artist vs. society **theme**, concluding that where society is the victim in Whiting's drama, it becomes the villain in Pinter's.

Hughes, C. "Pinter is as Pinter Does," Catholic World (December, 1969), 210:124-126.

Kahane, Eric. "Pinter et Le Realisme Irreel," L'Avant-Scene, No. 378 (April 15, 1967), 9, in French.

Dialogue and man's isolation are discussed.

Kalem, T. E. "Roomer," Time (October 12, 1970) 96:60+.

Kerr, Walter. "A Pox on Shocks," New York Times, II (January 15, 1967), 11:1.

Review of Pinter's *The Homecoming*.

____. Harold Pinter, No. 27 in the series "Columbia Essays on Modern Writers," New York and London, 1967.

Pinter not only states existential themes, his plays "function according to existential principle," Kerr asserts.

____. "Theater is the Victim of a Plot," New York Times, VI (June 25, 1967), 10.

Kerr speaks on the theatre as mostly unchanging though Pinter (especially in *The Homecoming*) is getting away from the conventional.

____. "The Theater: Pinter's Homecoming," New York Times, (January 6, 1967), 29:1.

Unfavorable report on *The Homecoming*.

Kitchen, Laurence. *Drama in the Sixties: Form and Interpretation*, London, 1966.

____. Mid-Century Drama, London, 1962.

"Compressionism" is seen as Pinter's main technique in both language and dramatic situation. Mentions similarity to Chekhov.

____. "**Realism** in the English Mid-Century Drama," World Theatre, XIV (January, 1965), 17-26.

A tracing of influences on contemporary English realists, citing a mastery of experimental staging, scenery, and dialect as praiseworthy and unprecedented graces.

Knight, G. Wilson. "The Kitchen Sink: On Recent Developments in Drama," Encounter, XXI (December, 1963), 48-54.

Pinter, as a member of the "kitchen sink" school of dramatists is depicted as trying to reestablish human values by balancing "mental discontinuities" with "objective absurdities."

Lahr, John. "Pinter and Chekhov: The Bond of Naturalism," The Drama Review, XIII (1968), ii:137-145.

____. "Pinter the Spaceman," Evergreen Review, No. 55 (June, 1968). Reprinted in Up Against the Fourth Wall, New York, 1969.

_____. A Casebook on Harold Pinter's *The Homecoming*, Copyright 1971 by Grove Press, Inc.

Leech, Clifford. "Two Romantics: Arnold Wesker and Harold Pinter," Contemporary Theatre, XX (1962), 11-31.

Leech feels that Pinter and Wesker share with Wordsworth and Coleridge and themselves a similar view and approach to the inner and outer life of a of man.

Levedova, I. "A New Hero Appears in the Theatre," Inostrannaya Literatura, No. 1 (January, 1962), 201-208, in Russian.

Pinter (Osborne, Wesker, Behan, Delaney) has created a protesting plebian hero.

Marines, Marya. "Just Looking, Thanks," Reporter, XXIII (October 13, 1960), 48.

"Pinter's talent lies as much in his silences as in his talk: his timing is masterly, his dialogue hypnotic in its repetition either of absurd cliches or plain human confusion."

Marowitz, Charles. "New Wave in a Dead Sea," Quarterly Review, I (October, 1960), 270-277.

Comments on Pinter, the most important of the "New Wave" dramatists, to the effect that his poetic drama depends on symbols and "mood concept" to "bypass the cerebrum and plunge directly into the [non-Freudian] psyche."

_____. "Notes on the Theater of Cruelty," Tulane Drama Review, XI (Winter, 1966), 152-156.

Artaud's "Theatre Cruelty" and its effect on young playwrights.

_____. "'Pinterism' is Maximum Tension Through Minimum Information," New York Times, VI (October 1, 1967), 36.

Generally a character sketch of Pinter, with some relating of facts of plays, especially the early ones.

_____. "Theatre Abroad," The Village Voice (September 1, 1960).

Pinter is questioned about the meaning of The Caretaker, which he claims is "about love" - which Marowitz equates with "need."

Mast, G. "Pinter's Homecoming," Drama Survey (Spring, 1968), 6:266.

Morris, Kelly. The Homecoming, Tulane Drama Review, XI (Winter, 1966), 185-191.

The Homecoming is seen as a sort of comedy of manners in the tradition of Ibsen and Strindberg combined with the aggressive nature of the family and a confusion of sexual roles.

Nadel, Norman. A Pictorial History of the Theatre Guild, New York, 1969.

Includes an illustrated account of the 1967 Broadway production of The Homecoming, a review of the criticism (including Nadel's own thoughtful and favorable remarks), and information about the play on tour.

Pallavincini, Roberto. "Aspetti della drammaturgia contemporanea," Aut Aut, No. 81 (May, 1964), 68-73, in Italian.

Failure to fulfill the social function of drama in terms of audience involvement.

Parker, R. B. "The Theory and Theatre of the Absurd," Queen's Quarterly, LXXIII (Autumn, 1966), 421-441.

Pinter (Beckett, Ionesco, and Genet) never "negates negation" to conform to the theory of the Absurd advanced by Camus in The Myth of Sisyphus.

Pesta, John. "Pinter's Usurpers," Drama Survey, VI (Spring, 1967), 54-65.

In Pinter's dramas, from *The Room* through *The Homecoming*, man's existential security is threatened by a "usurper."

PINTER, HAROLD

Plays:

The Birthday Party, London, 1959.

The Birthday Party and Other Plays, London, 1960. Also contains *The Room* and *The Dumb Waiter*.

The Caretaker, London, 1960.

A Slight Ache and Other Plays, London, 1961.

Also contains A Night Out, The Dwarfs, and the revue sketches "Trouble in the Works," "The Black & White," "Request Stop," "Last to Go," and "Applicant."

The Birthday Party and *The Room*, New York, 1961.

The Caretaker and *The Dumb Waiter*, New York, 1961.

Three Plays: A Slight Ache, The Collection, The Dwarfs, Grove Press, New York, 1962.

The Collection and *The Lover*, London, 1963. Also contains "The Examination."

The Homecoming, London, 1965; Grove Press, New York, 1967; London, 1968.

Tea Party and Other Plays, London, 1967. Also contains *The Basement* and *Night School*.

The Lover, Tea Party, The Basement, New York, 1967.

Landscape, London, 1968; Evergreen Review, No. 68, July, 1969.

A Night Out, Night School, Revue Sketches, Grove Press, New York, 1968. Also contains "Trouble in the Works," "The Black & White," "Request Stop," "Last to Go," and "Applicant."

"Landscape" and "Silence," London, 1969; Grove Press, New York, 1970. Also contains Night.

The Dwarfs and Eight Review Sketches, New York, 1965. Contains the revue sketches: "Trouble in the Works", "The Black & White," "Request Stop," "Last to Go," "Applicant," "Interview," "That's All," and "That's Your Trouble."

"Dialogue for Three," Stand, VI, No. 3, 1963.

"Special Offer," reprinted in Harold Pinter, by A. P. Hinchcliffe, New York, 1967, 73-74.

Movie Scripts:

The Servant (1962)

The Caretaker (*The Guest*) (1963)

The Pumpkin Eater (1964)

The Quiller Memorandum (1966)

Accident (1967)

The Birthday Party (1968)

The Go-Between (1969)

The Homecoming (1971)

Other Writings:

Poems, London, 1968. Contains most of Pinter's poems which have appeared in periodicals with the exception of "Rural Idyll" and "European Revels" in Poetry London, No. 20, November, 1950, and "One a Story, Two a Death," in Poetry London, No. 22, Summer, 1951, which appeared under the name of "Harold Pinta."

"Beckett," in Beckett at Sixty. A Festschrift, London, 1967.

Mac, London, 1968. A brief reminiscence of Pinter's association with the Irish actor-manager Andrew McMaster.

Tea Party (a prose version), Playboy, January, 1965.

"Memories of Cricket," Daily Telegraph Magazine, May 16, 1969.

"Between the Lines," speech at the Seventh National Students Drama Festival, Bristol, Sunday Times (London), March 5, 1962, 25.

An important revelation by Pinter of his concepts of verification and the use of language and paralanguage, often for defense.

Manuscript notes and a page of the typescript of *The Homecoming* are reproduced in London Magazine, New Series No. 100, July/August, 1969.

"Writing for Myself," Twentieth Century, CLXVIII (February, 1961), 172-175.

Pinter comments of the difficulties of writing stage drama, the influence of his acting career on his playwriting, the realistic/non-realistic qualities of his writing, and his refusal to write political drama.

"Writing for the Theatre," Evergreen Review, No. 33 (1964), 80-82.

Translations:

The Room:

De Kamer, De Dienstlift, De Huisbewaarder, De Collectie, De Minnaar (Dutch), Amsterdam, 1966.

Also includes *The Dumb Waiter*, *The Caretaker*, *The Collection*, *The Lover*.

The Birthday Party:

Dodumgunu Partisi (Turkish), trans. Memet Fuat, 1965.

L'Anniversaire (French), trans. Eric Kahane, Paris, 1968.

Feliz Aniversario (Portuguese), trans. Artur Ramos and Jaime Salazar Sempaio, Lisbon, 1967.

Norozeniny and Navrat Domu (Czech), trans. Milan Lukes, "Svetlova Literatura," No. 4, 1966.

Die Geburtstagsfeier, Der stumme Diener, Das Zimmer, Die Zwerge (German), trans. Willy H. Thiem (revised), Hamburg, 1969.

The Dumb Waiter:

Bez Pogovora (Serbo-Croat), Avangardna Drama, Belgrade, 1964.

Mathissen (Swedish), trans. Lars Boran Caisson, I En Akt, ed. Ingvar Holm, Stockholm, 1966.

O Monte Cargas (Portuguese), trans. Luis de Stau Moneiro, Tempo de Teatro, No. 3, Lisbon, n.d.

A Slight Ache:

Un leggero malessere and Una Serata Fouri (Italian), trans. Laura del Bono and Elio Nissim, Teatro Uno, ed. L. Codignola, Turin, 1962.

The Caretaker:

El Conserje (Spanish), trans. Josefina Vidal and F. M. Lorda Alaiz, Teatro Ingles, **Madrid, 1966**.

El Cuidor, El Amante, El Montaplatas (Spanish), trans. Manuel Barbera, Buenos Aires, 1965.

Also includes *The Dumb Waiter*.

El Portero (Spanish), trans. T. R. Trives, "Primero Acto," January, 1962.

A Gondnok (Hungarian), trans. Tibor Bartos, Mai Angol Dramak, Budapest, 1965.

Vicevaerten (Danish), trans. H. C. Branner, Fredensborg, 1961.

Spravce (Czech), trans. Milan Lukes, Prague, 1965.

Il Gardiano e altri drammi (Italian), trans. Elio Nissim, Milan, 1962.

Also contains La ***Stanza*** and Il Calapranzi.

Der Hausmeister, Eine Nacht ausser Haus, Abendkurs, Ein leichter Schmerz (German), trans. Willy H. Thiem (revised), Hamburg, 1969.

A Night Out:

En Tur i Byen (Danish), trans. Klaus Rifbjerg, "En Tur i Byen-Modeme Englesk Dramatik i TV og Radio," Fredensborg, 1962.

The Collection:

La Collection and El Amante (Spanish), trans. Luis Escobar, Primer Acto, No. 83, 1967.

La Collection suivi de lAmant et de Le Gardien (French), trans. Eric Kahane, Paris, 1967.

The Lover:

Kochanek (Polish), trans. B. Taborski, "Dialog," No. 8, 1966.

The Homecoming:

Le Retour (French), trans. Eric Kahane, L'Avant-Scene, No. 378, April 15, 1967.

Navrat Domu (Czech), trans. Milan Lukes, "Svetlova Literatura," No. 4, 1966.

Powrot do Dumo (Polish), trans. Adam Tarn, "Dialog," No. 12, 1965.

Die Heimkehr, Der Liebhaber, Die Killektion, Teegesellschaft, Tiefparterre (German), trans. Willy H. Thiem, Hamburg, 1967.

Landscape and Silence:

Dramen (German), trans. Renate and Martin Esslin, Hamburg, 1970.

Also includes Der Hausmeister, Eine Nacht ausser Haus, Abendkurs, and Ein Leichter Schmerz.

"Profile: Playwright on His Own," anon., Observer (September 15, 1963), 13.

An early biographical sketch is included in this quick summary of Pinter's playwriting and screenwriting up to *The Lover* and *The Dwarfs*.

Roll-Hansen, Diderik. "Harold Pinter og det absurde drama," Samtiden, LXXIV (September, 1965), 435-440, in Norwegian. Influences on Pinter of European dramatic traditions.

Rubens, Robert. "Donald McWhinnie," Transatlantic Review, No. 12 (Spring, 1963), 34-38.

An actor who has played in several of Pinter's works, McWhinnie, discusses Pinter's use of language.

Salem, Daniel. Harold Pinter, Dramaturge de l'ambiguite, Paris, 1968, in French.

Smith, Cecil. "Pinter: the Compulsion of Playwrighting," Los Angeles Times (December 3, 1967), Calendar Section, 1 and 19.

Pinter discusses his playwriting.

____. "Pinter's *The Homecoming* Opens," Los Angeles Times, IV, 1 and 9.

A review of *The Homecoming*, including an interpretation of the characters.

States, Bert O. "The Care for Plot in Modern Drama," Hudson Review, XX (Spring, 1967), 49-61.

Attacks Pinter's formlessness and lack of linear plot (in answer to John Russell Brown's "Mr. Pinter's Shakespeare").

____. "Pinter's Homecoming: The Shock of Nonrecognition," Hudson Review (August, 1968), 21:474.

Storch, R. F. "Harold Pinter's Happy Families," Massachusetts Review (August, 1967), 8:703.

Taylor, John Russell. Anger and After, Baltimore, 1963, revised 1969.

Includes an important chapter on Pinter as a writer whose "unique eminence" entitles him to be studied by himself. A study of each play through Landscape which includes a discussion of Pinter's techniques (especially in relation to "casting doubt upon everything by matching each apparently clear and unequivocal statement with an equally clear and unequivocal statement of its contrary") which concludes that Pinter's work is the "most 'musical' [i.e., poetic] of the new British drama."

____. Harold Pinter, No. 212 in Longman's "Writers and Their Work" series, London, 1969.

The study traces Pinter's development (up to and including Landscape, Silence, and Night) from the comedies of menace to the questions of identity and verification explored in the later plays.

Walker, Augusta. "Messages from Pinter," Modern Drama, X (May, 1967), 1-10.

Divides Pinter's work into allegories about life and cosmic concerns on the one hand and an examination of the drives within relationships between individuals.

Wellwarth, George. The Theater of Paradox and Protest, New York, 1964.

Pinter's "Comedy of Allusiveness" is reminiscent of the French avant-garde. By the time he had written *The Lover*, Pinter had established himself as "the most promising of England's young playwrights" with his "most original mind" and willingness to "experiment with new dramatic forms and techniques."

Williams, Raymond. Drama from Ibsen to Brecht, London, 1968.

Selected Reviews:

The Homecoming:

Guardian. March 27, 1965.

Daily Express. April 3, 1965.

Manchester Evening News. April 3, 1965.

Guardian. June 5, 1965.

New Statesman, 69:928. June 11, 1965.

Spectator. June 11, 1965.

New Republic, 152:29-30. June 26, 1965.

New Yorker, 41:50. June 31, 1965.

Encore. July-August, 1965.

Vogue, 146:75. September 15, 1965.

Time, 89:43. January 13, 1967.

New Yorker, 42:48. January 14, 1967.

Newsweek, 69:93. January 16, 1967.

Saturday Review, 50:51. January 21, 1967.

Nation, 204:122. January 23, 1967.

Commonweal, 85:459. January 27, 1967.

Reporter, 36:46. February 23, 1967.

Christian Century, 84:276. March 1, 1967.

Life, 62:6. March 3, 1967.

America, 116:353. March 11, 1967.

Hudson Review, 20:105-107. Spring, 1967.

Commentary, 43:73-4. June, 1967.

Additional Interviews:

Interview with John Sherwood, B.B.C. European Service, in "The Rising Generation" series, dated March 3, 1960.

Interview with Hallam Tennyson, B.B.C. General Overseas Service, August 7, 1960.

Interview with Kenneth Tynan, B.B.C. Home Service, recorded August 19, 1960, broadcast October 29, 1960.

Interview with Carl Wildman and Donald McWhinnie, B.B.C. Network Three, in the "Talking of Theatre" series, March 7, 1961.

Interview with Laurence Kitchin and Paul Mayersberg, in "New Comment" on the B.B.C. Third Programme, October 10, 1963.

Interview with Marshall Pugh, "Trying to Pin Down Pinter," Daily Mail (London), March 7, 1964.

Interview with John Russell Taylor, Sight and Sound, Autumn, 1966.

Interview in The New Yorker ("Talk of the Town"), February 25, 1967.

Interview with Kathleen Tynan, "In Search of Harold Pinter," Part 1 in the Evening Standard (London), April 25, 1968; Part 2, April 26, 1968.

Interview with Michael Dean, B.B.C. TV, "Late Night Line-Up," reprinted in The Listener, March 6, 1969.

Interview with Joan Bakewell, B.B.C. 2 TV, September 11, 1969.

www.ingramcontent.com/pod-product-compliance
Lightning Source LLC
LaVergne TN
LVHW011716060526
838200LV00051B/2917